Postcards from the Abyss

Prose, poetry, and aphorisms

All you men,
who think or say
that I am
malevolent, or
misanthropic

Philip Traum

ISBN-13: 979-8-218-51333-7

Printed in the United States of America

Some names and identifying details have been changed to protect the privacy of individuals.

Table of Contents

iv

In loving memory of my father,
Richard S. Feldman -
and dedicated to myself

You've come in! How lovely.
Now make yourself comfortable.
You seem thirsty. Drinks will be here soon.

What is your name? No, no - not the one you were given. The
one you truly are. The one you ought have been given. Do you
know it? Would you know it if you heard it?
If I were to call you by it?

Off with your clothes! They will be washed thoroughly, and you
will be provided with new and more appropriate ones. Or you
can choose to demur. You can undress and remain naked, if you
wish. These things are, naturally, up to you.
In any case, let us proceed.

Ah! Libations have arrived!
Drink deeply of the drink you hitherto dared not drink.
For here there shall be no talk of Lady Gagas
and Kim Kardashians - of gossip, of that which constitutes the
vast majority of human endeavor and thought,
of the dreary doings of the godforsaken day -
endlessly rehearsed, reiterated, and ruminated upon.
Here we speak only of beings and of things of consequence -
like me, and like you. Of night, of passion, and of dream.

Begin reading, and listen attentively to the voice within you, the
one who is reading now, the watcher,
who has been within and beside you for lo these many years -
always, since before you were born.
You, yet not you, because so very much more than you.

Here I am!

No, over here!

Have you conceived? Can you conceive? Will you?
There are more rooms in a box of snuff
than are generally assumed.

Let's find out, shall we?

Prologue: The girl and the spider - a love story

An unstained girl at the window, clear as glass,
Wipes the candled sleep from her moist eyes,
As she spies again the spider in the old oak tree.

Her Mum it was she asked,
Careful curious and apple-warm,
"Who is he really then, Mother, in our garden now,
With his berry-brushed eyebrows and spectacles,
His as-if eyes and puzzled smile? Do you know?
I remember him with me in the forceped room,
And I know he sits beside me still, silently,
In the drudged schoolroom of my dread-foolish days.
I shall approach him now, as lover and disciple,
Flesh-scrubbed and clothed in His lamb-red grace.
I know this, Mother, as I know scant else.
He returns for love and need of me."

"You are to sense return, child.
Such things are to be discussed neither by you
Nor by those who bleeding bore you.
You may follow the path of your fast-blooming lust,
But you are not to speak of it within these walls again.
And guard well the girlish fantasies in your rum-blood heart."

As she approaches, the spider glances sheepish towards her,
Dressed sack-clothed, and seeming ashen.
He'd walked, wishful and beauty-starved,
Through countless ghost-lit villages,
Through the belly of the weary and crusted earth
To this rigged and oiled dwelling
In the shadowed valley of her birth,
Where bells tolled and tears welled
When she'd butted her hairless head through mothered maw
In the blinding glare to faint and half-hearted applause.
Through spotted windows of latticed dream

He'd watched her ticking weary,
While all the while clinging long-full to the drooped and rusted
gutters,
Through snarled parks to yellowed buses
On the silent skirts of shrieking playgrounds.

Now he sits on his oaken throne,
Tapping timid and smiling strange,
A fitful meeting of flustered equals in the squalid garden of
hope.

Timid now she speaks,
"Kindest, gentlest spider,
If voiceless you are, sing otherwise to me.
As it suits you, it shall me.
There is surely more to you than kindest witness and solace,
And I would know it, now."

"I am but a tired, old spider,
Long undone and broken foolish under the lonely weight of
years.
You are young, sturdy-strong as the breast-boned oak on which I
sit,
And already grown wise."

"You see what you would, kind Spider.
Though my flesh is young, I am as ever
Sunken cruel-ish under a broken fate of tears.
If you love me, as I love you,
Tell me heaven's well-hid reason for my many births.
Mingle-marry and merge with me,
So that we might sit, double-backed and bestial,
At the blackened feet of the dark-stained Savior."

"Wisdom there is none in life's filth-muddled schoolyard.
All the lonelier and more helpless do I become
With each day passed and skin shed.
Do not ask these things of me, my child."

"Can you not teach me who I am, then?
Or give me peace?
Ravish me such that I might be unstuck
From this weary-wounded self for all time?
Must you deny me both history's solace and heaven's bliss?"

"God will deny you neither

(touching her cheek, then kissing her forehead...)

Though our love be eternal unto death and beyond,
Salted tears must sever now our precious earthly bond.

(gently tolling bells in the veiled distance...)

God calls me now to I know not where,
Calls to me kind through the cool night air.
Think on me, child, now fate pulls us apart,
My life soon to end and yours yet to start,
And sing to me, child, once you're snug and inside,
Songs that tell how we've lived and died.
Sing to me now of our lifelong love,
Of our many many lives-long love,
Of our oft-shattered hearts that are then made whole,
Of the love that binds us soul to soul,
Merged in bliss and turned to dust
In a fiery marriage bed of lust
That burns our flesh right up till when
We die and then are born again."

He quickly creeps from the tree
To scuttle swiftly through the hedges
To the tendrilled fields now to urn his keep
As she turns herself towards her trail of tears.

(wet as loins and dry as echoes)

Mother-frowns mount in the molten gloom
As the clock ticks tense and the door screams shut.
The ghostly hum and the spectral glow
Of the old TV in the short-lived room
Where the chimney smoke makes its swift escape
Pushing mad over crested hills
To rasping smack against buried steeples.

(For now she remains a wisping girl,
Though her destiny be the wide world's bellows.)

He had borne this death,
He had lived this loss,
He'd endured this pain many times before,
Though the cast was diff'rent
And the scene was changed,
He'd watched countless times as she'd closed that door.

Opens she now the latticed glass,
The windowed bars of her frozen pain
To bare her soul in a newborn song
Which warms the earth like a summer rain...

Though his legs grew weary
And his eyes grew tired,
And he feared there'd be on trouble on his journey long,
His gait grew merry
And his smile grew wider
When the breeze caressed him with her fragrant song.

As her song echoed fragrant 'neath the star-struck moon,
He weaved around its melody a second tune -

"We shall one day embrace and become one another,
With our limbs crisscrossed and face to face
In the womb of the universal Mother
On her milk-white throne in the star-flung place...,

(As the spider slowly scuttles from the reader's sight...,)

And cradled in the galaxies of deepest space...

(Their song goes fading gentle into that good night.)

By the blessed gift eternal of our Father's grace..."

FINIS

A diminutive cacophony of grandiose balderdash and pomposity

The things that bind us to physicality straitjacket us - hunger, lust - these things weigh us down, and bind us to earth. There are other sources of nourishment constantly hovering all around us, just out of our reach. If I were to smash the piano, rip up my birth certificate, and fast for three weeks in solitude, what would become of me? This "me" that teaches piano to a few wonderful, but mostly snot-nosed children and annoying adults, comes home, late at night, to listen to messages on his answering machine - that guy. "That guy" is a very bad, ill-fitting garment - exchangeable, and illusory. What is that primordial sound? The one which we hear both in the late quartets of Beethoven, and in the horrible cackle which emanates from the smoke-infested lungs and larynx of some ancient crone, dying of cancer in a public hospital, and abandoned by her family? There is this other way to know. Everything in ordinary life - every relationship, every aching need, every pitiful grasping - all these things are distractions, opiates, time wasters. I feel this in my bones, but I can't quite get to it. I can almost touch it. Perhaps asceticism and solitude are paths towards it. Although lustful gluttony might just as likely be effective. And lustful gluttons are ever so much more fun.

I've been thinking about the way the "text' is venerated as some sort of "divine emanation" from or through the composer by classical musicians, as if what successive generations thought or think about it are not relevant. They're more than relevant - they're the crux of what the damned thing means. As if having, or having seen, an autograph copy of such and such a work might give one the doctrinal status of some sort of priest. What if the composer's mind changed when the thing was on the way to the printer, after a hearty meal with plenty of garlic, or a spat with a lover? What if a near-infinite host of circumstantial stuff had not conspired to produce the "work" in such and such a manner, at such and such a time? To ignore the contingency of absolutely everything is to willfully ignore reality. When we listen to a "work" a sufficient number of times, we become convinced it must be "just so" and not otherwise, but this is just our extremely stupid, lower nature, the part of us that cannot escape moronic religious "truths" beaten into our heads as children, the conditioned part of us. Yes, 98% of folks are sheep. I'm not talking to those folks at the moment. The word "work" is a monumental misnomer, unless you understand it as a verb, as a process. I'm no philosopher. Innit obvious? But I do know that once the thing, once anything, is written in stone, it's dead. I heard a conductor, a very well-known conductor, who should have known better, because he was a jazz pianist in a previous incarnation, say that once his interpretation is arrived at, it never changes, it might only, hopefully, deepen. Huh? And yet this is clearly the way in which many admittedly great men have lived, worked, composed, and performed. But had we the opportunity to hear Chopin play Bach - would we rather hear Chopin be "true to the composer", or true to himself?

I walked the dogs for over an hour. If only I could be like them for a moment - a nanosecond would suffice. Time and space would come apart, fear would disappear - all my future-oriented, hypothetical apprehensions and anxieties would disappear. Who can be like that? No one.

There is no moral dimension to the universe. There's a love of play, a love of creation, and, without question, a love of destruction. Men get drunk on creating, and blood-drunk in their lust to destroy. Freud is probably right about the invention of morality. What to make of the sort of altruism displayed by mothers sacrificing themselves for their country, or poor, misguided schmucks taking the sword for their country? What is that? It is some sort of intuitive understanding, amongst all of us, the rabble no less than those few-and-far-between higher beings, that we are not finite, that we don't end at the boundaries of our skin. What could be a clearer demonstration of this than mob behavior?

I would like to have the strength of solitude, of self-knowledge, and self-reliance. I have only the strength of, and frequent wish for, the first. I would like to possess those other things, yet still be able to care and be out and about amongst people, but I don't know that I'm capable of that, certainly not now. Perhaps I never was. I despise the world I live in - its seemingly endless, frivolous, and distracting entertainments, its deep ennui and cynicism, its fear, its greed, its inexhaustible supply of stupidity. I despise these things most of all in myself.

I think that jazz far more accurately reflects the workings of the world around us - in a more legitimate way than the Western canon, with its orthodox "works". Jazz music, well, it's all over - at the very least, it "smells funny". Yet it did, at one time, have an evolving language, perfected in hothouse atmospheres of intense competition, the sharing of ideas, and the honing of one's craft - it was the highest embodiment of folk art. The "piece"didn't matter one bit - only one's contribution to the endless stream, the endless, evolving, present-tense current. That current was shifted, different, and new the instant one's contribution was made - from moment to moment, performance to performance, day to day. Of course, this is also true of the Goldberg Variations, and how we think of them now, ca. 300 years, and many millions of performances, later. There is no "Goldberg Variations", as Bach wrote them. But no one can admit this obvious fact. They pretend the "Goldberg Variations" descended from on high, and that any and all traditions are encrustations or dilutions of its original, pristine, Godlike, "Platonic-Idea" essence. Nonsense. Even the Jews understand this. They wrote the Talmuds, after all, and understand that the Bible is enriched and made new by such commentary. This is somewhat true, I suppose, of rock 'n' roll, but the musical language is so dreadfully impoverished, and the sentiments so dreadfully one-dimensional, that who cares, really. Needless to say, all that "moon and June" bullshit of Tin Pan Alley was pure rubbish as well, although the tunes were WAY better. But jazz isn't about any of that anyway. It's about divine play, process - an evolving communal language that everyone contributes to, the great ones and the also-rans alike. Too bad it's all finished. "Classical Music" had a run like that, as well. Of course, the moment it was deemed "Classical Music", that was its death knell. It was finished and spent by the time of old Richard Strauss, Schönberg, Berg, Webern, etc. The Four Last Songs really were "The Four Last Songs". The coffin was sealed. It now staggers around like a blindfolded zombie in an overpriced morgue, demanding respect, like some godforsaken relative at a holiday get-together, whose face you'd like to bash in.

The baby boomers are convinced the world should give a damn about their problems and be profoundly thankful for their utterly inconsequential contributions to culture. Can one imagine a more nauseating bunch? "Classic rock " - there's a good joke. Rock 'n' roll did revolt against a certain, stilted formalism, which was beginning to make the world of popular music feel claustrophobic. That's all well and good, but what did it offer in its place? What did Philip Glass offer us when serialism, et al. was spent and in its death throes? The beginnings of some new tradition that could develop? That had SOME content, even if the beginnings of the journey on that new road were relatively primitive? What it did, in the case of rock 'n' roll, was to cynically steal the traditional, legitimate, and sincerely created folk music of black people for purely commercial purposes. And if you just repeat that crap over and over sufficiently, and market it as if it's meaningful - if critics write glowing hymns of praise to Mick Jagger, as if he mattered in any way, except in the obvious, icky ways - as an icon of a blasted culture, a cynical creation of the popular media - a whole generation will buy into the scam. Liszt was a revolutionary. He changed the course of music history, of performance, of harmony - perhaps not for the better, who am I to say. However, he spent his whole youth in endless practice, study, and the absorption of a tradition which he then messed with, even smashed to pieces towards the end, or "extended", depending on your point of view. It was a deep tradition and it belonged to him. What rock 'n' roller can make this claim? What filmmaker can? I suppose there are, perhaps, a few filmmakers who can.

I feel something - something awful, terrible, just out of my grasp - pressing in and down on my consciousness, something implicit in everything around me - strangely and serenely beyond me, beckoning. It gives me a headache.

Alice

She took the seat directly in front of mine in my 11th grade Social Studies class. It was, perhaps, fate. She changed my life, irrevocably and forever. Alice.

She was new to my high school, and had just transferred from a town which was somewhat lower-class, hence less pretentious, entitled and God-awful than was my own, some ten or twelve miles away. She came without prejudice - utterly benign, and as yet unaware of just whom it would be in her best interests to pursue. She was an outsider, by simple definition, and, as such, divine, precious. An outsider, like me.

Alice was shy, and terribly insecure about where her place in this new environment was and ought to be. She was superficially extroverted, yet, at the same time, deeply shy, mysterious, and anxious. I watched her pull chunk after chunk out of her lovely brown hair, nervously and compulsively, as I sat behind her, lost in my adolescent fantasies and longings.

The fact of her ample bosom was hardly lost on me, although, at my tender age, and with my lack of experience, her breasts were as frightening as they were fascinating

She quickly procured a boyfriend for herself - Dan. He moved in the same embarrassingly naïve, countercultural circles as I - the faux-hippie (which, I suppose, is an oxymoron), music-loving and playing, pot-smoking circles. He struck me as sorely lacking in misfit and outcast credentials, and was a transparently misplaced, unwelcome interloper - a future Young Republican. But of course I needed to hate him. He was "balling" (his word - a word that made me sick with frustrated anger and sadness) the girl with whom I was to have the greatest intimacy of my young life, and with whom I was already in love.

Whether I was physically attracted to Alice was not entirely clear to me. I hadn't the experience, nor the introspective skills, to be sure. I had the recurrent magical thought that it would somehow be ill-advised for me to masturbate while thinking of her. I mustn't, since there was some vanishingly remote chance I might one day have some actual sexual contact with her. From my perspective now, this is, needless to say, ludicrous. At the time, it somehow made sense.

I knew that she was kind, and that her smile haunted me, day and night, through my long days of longing, and in dream. Her femininity seemed more maternal or sisterly, than purely, or in any way overtly, sexual. The latter might very well have overwhelmed and intimidated me to the point where communication might have become impossible.

We passed silly notes back-and-forth. We were pals. She was gentle, accepting, and warm. It was idyllic, that is until my nemesis would appear on the stage. When she was with Dan, their togetherness had a staged quality - a posed, high school yearbook, "Look at us! We are definitely a couple, aren't we?" feel to it. It was obvious to me, at least, that she and I were far more right for one another. My friends, the three or four who were really my friends, were sympathetic to my dilemma, and understood, to some extent, what my knowing Alice had come to mean to me, although my friend Malcolm was either unwittingly, or wittingly, sufficiently sadistic to let me know that his mom had asked him whether I was homosexual, given that I hadn't had a girlfriend by what seemed to her this late date in my life. Thanks, pal.

Oh, those horrid, humiliating times! They were the purest torture - comparing one's progress through puberty with other young men in the forced nakedness of the swimming pool locker room. I feared I was asexual (well, not exactly true, I thought about little else besides touching naked women). What I actually feared was that I would never be skilled, lucky, or brave enough to negotiate the opportunity to touch a naked woman.

A year or two previously, Elaine Zorn had pulled me down on the hotel bed on which we had been sitting, on the very last night of an obscene "Teen Tour" for snot-nosed, over-privileged brats, on which my parents had sent me. Why? Because this is what their neighbors did, and "when in Rome", etc. It's the only reason I was bar mitzvahed, as well. Elaine's intention was, obviously, to kiss me. I involuntarily pulled away out of sheer terror, and devised some bit of silliness, which now escapes me, to excuse my not responding. We were in a room with other people. I was insanely attracted to her. If God existed, surely one could and would find Him resting contentedly in that precociously large and freckled teenage cleavage of hers. Here was the opportunity of my young life, up until that point, and I bugged out. This seemed to me proof that my future was to contain little else other than loneliness and sexual deprivation. The fruit had fallen off the tree, right into my famished lap, and I couldn't bring it to my lips to taste it.

Alice was barely five-feet tall, ten or fifteen pounds overweight, very buxom (as I am aware I have already mentioned) and with the sweetest face, kindest eyes, and loveliest smile one could imagine. A fairy-tale, little peanut girl - charming, cute, delightful. My parents adored her - even my mother, the harpy from Hell, seemed to like her. My dad was especially fond of her. At that time, he still possessed the emotional intelligence, mental faculties, and intuitive gifts of which time, drugs, and booze have since robbed him. He saw her depth, her nobility, her uniqueness, and found her quite extraordinary.

Dan went away that summer to some capitalist training seminar, or pre-corporate boot camp. And so it was that Alice and I were together constantly. We spent long, languorous nights in Queens Point Park, lying side-by-side, in endless magical conversation - never touching, drinking one another in with our eyes. Did we build a fire? I can't remember. Perhaps. I do remember that I never felt frustrated lying next to her through those many enchanted nights - just a cosmic rightness, a happiness, a gratitude. Trees, breeze, moonlight, her silvery-sweet voice. We might have smoked pot a couple of times. I don't know. I do know that nothing mattered except her. I can't recall a single thing we talked about, though we did talk, endlessly - only that it was effortless. Boundaries dissolved, souls merged. On that last night of the summer, with Dan about to return, when we both knew these special nights were soon to end, she unzipped my pants and touched me. I can't recall if we kissed or not. I do know that I blurted out "I love you" many times, in rapid, needy succession. My heart was bursting. I tear up now, recalling it.

We didn't return until the next morning. Both sets of parents had called the police. They'd been out looking for our bodies in all the neighborhood pools. My parents showed no joy upon my returning home alive, only vitriolic anger, and had apparently extensively ruminated-upon plans for how I was to be punished. But no chastisement could possibly touch me at that point. I had tasted life, I had rolled it around on my tongue and could savor it still, if only in memory.

I recall half expecting the sky to have turned some new and heretofore unseen color, in honor of this, my first sexual experience. The world did seem, in a certain way, fresh and new, although I also remember it simultaneously seeming as if it were decidedly apathetic as regards my internal chatter, with all of its adolescent, emotional hyperbole.

The pain of the next few months was exquisite. Notes passed in homeroom - "Hank, sweet Hank, you are torturing my soul...." Anguished expressions, averted, downcast gazes. I feel them still. They sit alongside all the other wretched soul-agonies I later experienced with perhaps a half-dozen other women, at times becoming confused, or simply meshing with them.

I loved Alice very much - very, very much. I can never repay her for awakening me to a new, hallucinatory world of passion, intimacy, and volcanic emotion. I can see you now, Alice - you are perfectly vivid before me, and yet, at times, your features become blended with the features of other women, some of whom mattered, others who did not. It's as if I peer into a place where there is only one, primal, undifferentiated Woman, who has, at various times, nurtured, abandoned, and attempted to destroy me - to whom I cry out in longing in my sleep, and who repeatedly stabs and mutilates me with her eternally recurring abandonments and betrayals.

I remember once, in bed, in her pitch-black dorm room, Alice moaned the word "Come" to me when I was inside her - either in a moment of passion, or, perhaps, of let's-get-it-over-with impatience. My hyperactive imagination immediately transformed her - dropping her voice several registers, and metamorphosing her into a hungry, hairy demon-beast, whose violent embrace clearly spelled danger. I flew out of the bed in a heartbeat, and turned the light on in terror.

Dear God - it was like those times when, as a small boy, I would imagine that, the moment I closed the door, my parents would immediately regain their true bodily form, that of witches, monsters. I was their helpless little experiment. Whenever I was in their presence, they, of course, behaved as if they were my "human" parents. I could not surprise them, reveal them, make public their gruesome secret - no door could be thrown open with sufficient swiftness to achieve that. I had no human parents, no siblings, no kin, no ancestors. I was a thing adrift, washed up on the shore as a science project for some alien civilization. Whether they were evil or not, I wasn't entirely sure, although my choice of metaphor for who they actually were, behind closed doors, would seem to imply that I thought them deeply evil. That they were profoundly different, estranged, and remote from me, of this I was sure. They could not even remotely fathom, love, or empathize with me.

I had potency problems with Alice at first. I can remember often losing my erection in the few seconds just before penetrating her those first few weeks. If, by some stroke of luck, I was able to make it inside of her, before my paranoia could overwhelm me, my fears and misgivings would disappear, and some more or less healthy, adolescent banging would ensue. It was during that moment when I would attempt to enter her, of some part of me deciding whether I would allow myself to be that vulnerable, that my panic stricken-ego would retreat to the sidelines, defeated. My amygdala, traumatized by God knows what and whom, would then emerge from the psychic sludge, like the Loch Ness monster, to shrivel up my dick to the size of a baby corn.

I slept with Alice in her bed in her tiny double room at Rhode Island University, three feet away from her stocky, infinitely patient, Irish roommate, Katie, who really should, from that day forward, be referred to as Saint Katie, from my present vantage point, for putting up with that shit.

Alice and I were equals. She was my friend-lover. I have no memory, or real sense of what our sex was like. I certainly had nothing to compare it to. If there was a man-woman dynamic, it was secondary to the genuine, and very nourishing feeling of being best friends.

In my junior year of college, she began mentioning a fellow whom she very much wanted me to meet, or at least to observe surreptitiously. All my paranoid instincts came to the fore. And they were correct. I knew what she was trying to tell me. One doesn't need all that much previous experience to make some very basic and obvious deductions in life. But I ignored all the warnings, even if I did, at some level, dimly foresee the emotional holocaust to come.

I remember that horrendous, soul-crushing night as if it were yesterday - my endless interrogations, the final discovery that she had even brought her diaphragm with her to his apartment, fully intending to sleep with him. I ran off into the blackness, like a wounded animal, howling and disoriented. How I found myself inserting coins into a payphone at 5:30 the next morning I shall, perhaps, never recall. The caring voice of she, who had stayed up all night, guilty and terrified, and who picked up the phone after one ring, I shall never forget.

An Angel of Death

An Angel of Death shoves a poisoned IV
In the comatose body of a once living God -
Let the Devil come in 'fore your time runs out,
And boink loose change with your divining rod.

On sunny streets ain't no hoodies allowed -
If you sweat while you work, you are likely to die -
Though I seemed to survive till my summer vacation,
And then thought of you - who the hell knows why.

What do you want, and what do you dream of?
And when will you make all your sins up to me?
You're a lying dog, and a filthy scoundrel -
PLEASE go away, and just leave me be.

I'm the Almighty God of a store-bought ant farm,
The subject of pious, invertebrate prayer -
I live for the moment, but when that's gone and dead,
I'll be stuffed down a hole in my underwear.

I sit at the window, and wait for the sunrise -
Things have grown quiet on the Western Front -
I bleed for my country, and laugh at my rivals -
I'm my Momma's pride, but my litter's runt.

Enough with this rhyming, this new formalism -
It's for overstuffed children, or entitled Professors
Impaled on broomsticks, of poisonous hellcats
Who are looking for action at New Jersey truck stops

Where I'm fucked up the ass by some mindless eternity,
And dancing Mazurkas with Alex Trebek -
Which is natural for me, since I'm three-quarters Polish -
And which parts are those? Pray tell us! Which parts?

The parts with no honor, which bend over backwards
To rat on his neighbors, as a matter of course -
The parts that hurl breakfasts at Latvian waitresses,
Mustached and bleating in local church choirs -
Who's known for extortion, and insider trading...
Well that's what Der Stürmer says, what do I know.

I would sext constantly, if I just knew
How to cop a damned iPhone, and get on the web -
I've the apple of temptation in my eye like a floater,
And the pear of frustrations up my ass like a shoe.

I'm a hemorrhoidal ointment in an upscale shop,
A hairy-ass crotch, in a Photoshop world -
I don't make what a hardworking Grecian urns
Writing theremin ditties for Star Trek conventions

Where dead test-tube babies play air-brushed guitars,
On which static is clinging to Heidi Klum's snatch -
In which Ken Jennings lies on a long bed of nails,
And odious folks such as I aren't allowed.

Astonish me -
For I have seen things no mortal could conceive of,
Much less admit to.
I've got a ticket to ride
Roughshod over your feelings,
To trip up your plans
For more days than you'd care to imagine -
To make sacrificial victims of your most prized possessions -
To cook cabbage rolls over your burning books,
While trimming your deformed puppy's nails -
To cross my fingers, and hope to die -
Though dying is easy,
It's the living that's hard.

18

Verwende wieder Reime, du Idiot! Das ist schmerzhaft!

Ok, Ok -

To lie in a coma is no easy thing -
I'm a soft touch really, but I'm great in bed -
I make crosses from headboards, and set fires in caves -
No worries!
(I'll lower the prices when I raise the dead.)

Blow me a load, and hum me a horncall -
Sing me a song from your childhood -
Bury your wounded knees in the churchyard -
(And since it's quite clear that you're burnt out and jaded)
Take a leaf of absinthe - it'll do you good.

An incredible man

An incredible man has decidedly shrunken
To lengths which no bulls in the Orient go -
A minotaur weeps that his hourly wage
Is now stuck in a field, where no sunflowers grow.

In classical Greece, all the white wooden ships
Were sailed by a well-oiled Spartan brigade
For romantic liaisons with African slave girls,
Whose sensuous, glistening bodies they laid

For a ticket to heaven, or ticket to ride
In the back of a bus, at the front of the class -
All their pagan conceits, and promiscuous wiles
Couldn't get Plato to give them a pass

To the carnival booths, and the virulent sideshows,
Where the freaks and the geeks put their wares on display,
Selling olive-soaked bread to an ignorant rabble
While pedophile priests who were flagrantly gay

Took a cruise ship to Tripolis, bartered for boys,
Philosophized nude in the pale afternoon,
Discussed the ideal while displaying their crotches,
Then chewed on their nails, as they bayed at the moon.

Near the entrance to Hades, a man in a boat
Slips his soul through a keyhole, and mutters a prayer
For his nightmares to end, and his garments to shrink,
Once he tightens the noose, and then drop-kicks the chair

Down the hill, far enough so that even in Hades
Fair Charon has upped and abandoned his post -
Elysium snickers as Athens unravels,
And Persephone wails as she gives up the ghost.

Shrink-wrap your soul near a small basement window -
Outwit the spider, devour the night -
Melt in the mouth of a cave lit by fire,
While spirits get busy, and dance in the light

Of some deeply loved woman, or her Ideal Form -
Some feminine figure, who's tender and mild...
Or some monolith slab, where the meaning of Life's
In the loins of desire, or the eyes of a child.

An unwelcome collision with reality

I believe that this one session will suffice to give you what, in our circles, constitutes a diagnosis, Mr. <X>. We psychoanalysts do not deal in insurance-created labels and simple, flavor-of-the-week pronouncements, as you might have suspected. I will tell you the truth, as I see it, and I do - in a way that you, as a layman, can easily understand.

You are in such an infantile rage over your feelings of having been shortchanged by your parents that you have transformed your petty, bitchy, regressed fury into a religion of nihilism. Yes, yes - your parents abused you while simultaneously overprotecting you and stuffing you full to bursting with contradictory feelings of grandiosity, inferiority, and terror. That is not hard to see! Had it not ever occurred either to you, or to any of your previous therapists? Was there no one before me who saw all your anger for what it is? The sadism of a little boy who was subjected to disingenuous displays of affection which alternated, rapidly and unpredictably, with physical and psychological violence? A little boy who now, unsurprisingly, takes pleasure in torturing his peers? He's never quite sure why, only that it feels right, for they have all, somehow, even if he can't pinpoint or quantify that "somehow", wronged him. No matter - this dreadful feeling within him, these thousands of hatpins stuck long ago in his flesh, point unequivocally, in his mind, to their guilt. All of them, without exception. On rare occasions, the little boy encounters someone who seems sufficiently damaged and vulnerable that his milder instincts, his empathy, and, dare I say it, even his long ago crushed, castrated instinct to love is evoked. But this never lasts. It can never last. Why? Because there are no people who are simply that and nothing besides, simply "damaged and vulnerable", and hence dependably alluring. The moment this one-dimensionally "vulnerable" person's complexity begins to emerge, the project is abandoned, ending inescapably in displays of the little boy's fear or condemnation as regards the formerly potential love object, which was so deeply attractive just moments before. This little boy, who is so full of passions of all sorts, all of them sickly, mangled, and perverse - who, apparently, hasn't even begun to put $2 + 2$ together.

And so that little boy continues to seek out these vulnerable strangers, the ones whom he also knows, in addition to being initially appealing, will present no challenge, because that little boy also was, and remains, a coward. And as I said a moment ago, the denouement for him, and sometimes them, is always disastrous. He's always been, and is still, afraid to stick his neck out, to see if he has any talent worthy of being praised by those who would know perfectly well whether or not this is the case. He's afraid to go in the big boy pool, as it were. But then, why should he? When he can live the cloistered, grandiose life of the condescending, self-important, idealistic, I'm-a-legend-in-my-own-mind loner? So now we have both of those little boy's reasons, excuses, and defense mechanisms, both of which enable and encourage him to consistently choose to stick his head in the sand, and to live such a hopelessly circumscribed life - the house-of-cards safe haven, which he has taken great time and great care to construct, and his cowardice. You, you being that little boy, avoid it, in the end, because you have a way and lifestyle and inner familiar chatter which makes it possible, and because you are utterly unable to follow through on it because of your faintheartedness - it is simply too terrifying for you. And hence, as it has in the past and as it will continue to - everything inevitably crashes and burns, you retreat into the hurt and vitriolic posture of the wounded child, and you are, once again, submerged, by no one's hands other than your own, in a pool of hydrochloric acid, choking and gagging on your feelings of loneliness, inferiority, and self-loathing. All of your nobler, braver instincts (although the latter are in vanishingly short supply), as you see them, are revealed to be what they always were. A counterfeit fortress, erected against the real enemy, which is you, when you are forced to look at yourself honestly. But you cannot dare to linger there. You have not truly arrived at this Pogo-like state of self-awareness, not in any ongoing way, at any rate.

You see yourself as the cut-off point for the worthy vs. the worthless. You always have. Those to whom you feel superior are swine, lacking justification to draw breath - those to whom you feel inferior are terrifying - they hold the fearsome potential of doing you in with a single incisively pointed assessment. Those to whom you feel more or less equivalent are granted, in your mind, tentatively, but only tentatively, the right to exist. What kind of man is it that seeks every opportunity to keep risk and challenge at bay, who inevitably chooses the most expedient, comfortable course at every turn, and who is hyper-aware of doom, and constantly obsessing about that grim reaper of decay and death hovering behind him, and over him, at every moment? Who feels every compliment must be either an agenda-filled lie, or the confirmation of the stupidity of its giver? Who finds only rejection appealing and true? Yes, yes - your mother smothered you with praise you knew was a sham one moment, and then beat you down the next, literally and figuratively. And yet another person would have come out of all that very differently. You are made of very weak stuff, Mr. <X>.

And so you have developed, not consciously, but nevertheless quite meticulously, a kind of battle plan for life, for those times when you are forced to interact with the world at large. You operate from a very deep belief that if you can convince everyone that their ideals and priorities are lies and defenses, that then, and only then, when you have succeeded in chopping them down to your size, and they, of necessity, begin to feel what it is that you constantly feel, that they will then be able to join you where you are - in the void - the empty, lonely void in which you've existed for as long as you can recall, since your consciousness first winked into existence as a toddler - and that maybe, or so you fantasize, you might potentially have a basis on which to develop a real rapport with another human being. It is lonely living on the head of a pin, is it not, Mr. <X>? You are very accomplished at this chopping others down to size - chop, chop, chop! It feels good, yes? And you are quite accomplished at it! The truth is you'd be a very good cult leader, if you had charisma and something to offer these folks in return, hoax or no. But you haven't a shred of charisma. And it is far from clear that you have something, anything, to offer in return. And yet still, your goal is clear. You strive mightily to get these others to share your emptiness and despair. It is your fondest wish and goal. And you are sufficiently intelligent to realize that your tactical arsenal for achieving said goals are often insufficient - hence you are constantly reading, enlisting aid from the written words of other pessimists and nihilists, more intelligent pessimists and nihilists. And yet, you would throw all of that over in a heartbeat, if only you could stand next to a beautiful woman and feel her love, accept it, trust it, believe in it, drink it in. And, much, much more importantly than that, though equally impossible - if you could feel any sort of real love for her in return. Not just a hint of that love, which disappears the moment you are frightened or challenged. That you have felt many times. I'm referring to the real thing, experienced in an ongoing way. I'm afraid the potential for that was strangled long ago, perhaps in your very early years, more likely during your infancy, in your crib. The sad truth is that you will never see, have, or experience any of this. You will die a bitter, beaten dog.

By the way, now that we are speaking of dogs. You claim to love your dog, and I believe you. But it's very easy to love a dog. A dog is a pathetic, pea-brained creature who is nothing other than need, and quite incapable of discernment. We bred all good sense out of wolves long ago. What is left is a bucket into which we pour our projections - a sad, needy puppet we humans have created. You do have something of a heart for the vulnerable, the pathetic, those incapable of challenging or criticizing you. And, at some moments, even something resembling real empathy. Which we both know full well is only self-love by another name. But the moment this vulnerable love-object upon whom you are showering your projections, needs, and self-love speaks up for itself, shows a hint of independence, or, perish the thought, has the audacity to challenge you, even mildly, you either flee in terror, or unleash a torrent of unwarranted vitriol. This has been, and will always be, your character, the artificial fabric of your life. Were your dog to do so, to defy you, or to simply display some modest amount of independence, the result would be precisely the same. That you were betrayed, that you were cheated on by two of your significant girlfriends early in your romantic life is no surprise. You must have been asking for it. You might as well have worn a t-shirt advertising your naked, raw need, your hair-trigger rage at the slightest hint of rejection, your inability to trust, your expectation that you would be betrayed, and your misogyny.

We needn't see one another again. But do take care to recall - you're too frightened of death to consider suicide. You must remember your true nature - you are, first and foremost, a coward. And let us conclude on a final note of what has been, perhaps, my too ruthless honesty, for which I apologize, although I have found it very hard to refrain from it in your case - there is still so much bittersweet emptiness and sadism for you to taste before this Mr. Death arrives, over whom you constantly obsess - He who will one day either gradually or quite immediately rip your guts apart, and make you worm food. Don't you want to hang around and indulge yourself in this ongoing feast of barren solitude and savagery? It's the only food you ever had or ever will have a taste for. There always has been, and always will be, an abundance of these things at your table. Enjoy them.

Good day, Mr. <X>

Ancient Ode to a Momentary Flame

For Desiree

we speak here
dialects of narcissism -
with inflections
recognizable enough,
each to the other,
to devise
an effective,
bastard language.

no comfort here -
on this exquisite bed of nails,
upon which we weep
lacerated blood-tears:
you and i
will never
go gently
into that good night.

as you saunter,
languid,
upon the plush red carpet
unrolled beneath your feet,
you will,
perhaps,
forgive me -
and,
soothed
by the honeyed adulation
of those watery whisperings,
echoing,
in that seashell you hold,
fast,
to your ear,
you will forget.

hothouse flowers we -
overwrought,
perfumed,
who would wear,
in deepest night,
each other's selves
like skins -
aflame,
and veiled
in a dark cloak
of soulhunger,
sensation,
awe -
unfettered
by responsibility:
a kind of truth -
skins -
peeled,
and shed
at sunrise,
in exchange
for stale uniforms
of dawn,
when the world
of appearances
holds sway.

laughter is anesthesia -
day's remedy
for night's
terrible,
cathartic
cravings -
souls,
bound
in bittersweet
barbed wire -
vampiric ecstasy -

which day dissolves,
and betrays.

seek then
the reassuring smiles
and creature comforts
of day:
the cool drink,
the easy chair,
the warm,
lazy,
sunlit
afternoon.

and,
if,
on some cool,
innocuous evening,
a delicious hot breeze
slaps you in the face -
musky-scented,
enthralling -

causing tired blood
to tingle
like molten lava -
if,
then,
your glance
wanders towards the horizon,
where the moon
plummets earthwards,
id-drunk, raving -
do not linger there!
a warm, inviting supper
awaits you inside…

annie wong lived in a shitty cow-town

annie wong lived in a shitty cow-town
where girls like penny put her down
girls named june july and beulah
and badly acne-scarred talullah

her boyfriend tony was a pimp
whose money that he'd saved and scrimped
went to open a hair salon
and pay off his uncle the mafia don

she'd tried to shave though as he slept
she turned out being more adept
at gouging his cheeks with untrimmed nails
and tossing his flesh in garbage pails

(a dog is great on a warm spring day
if he doesn't bite and likes to play
though when he dies you will be crushed
ashes to ashes dust to dust)

annie wong died in the fall last year
though no one really shed a tear
and tony's swagger dropped three pegs
when his uncle shattered both his legs

tell your mama tell your pa
tain't nothin' like a hottie in a spandex bra
tell 'em you'd prefer to drown
than live in some pretentious town

where letters are all lower case
where fakery's shoved in your face
where language is so oft ill-used
that readers are left pissed confused

by poems like this one about annie
where one can search each nook and cranny
wondering what is intended
just 'cause it's been recommended

by some grizzled high-school teacher
some burnt-out, withered, mustached creature
(who - even though she whines and begs
you should still break both her legs)

Auf Wiedersehen für immer, du Stück Scheiße

This one left too. They all leave, only to be replaced by another - indistinguishable from the first. I might as well be a social insect, for all the importance individuality has had in my life. A monkey can love a wire hanger. Did you know that in the transference, monkeys re-experience their early years through their projections onto the therapist, who is also a wire hanger? Wire hangers have their place in life - it's a perfectly noble and dignified one. They made it easy for, and appealing to, Joan Crawford, to beat the living hell out of her fat, bloated, ungrateful daughter. Why, they have scraped the filth from the stinking uteri of poor, white trash women in fetid trailer park port-o-sans for generations! What's not to like? Not to mention that they are quite effective in ripping the skin from one's leg or arm - they make one feel, oh, so alive!

Fuck her, she's gone. She was a faceless simpleton. I'm so tired. I can't do this again. A hole is a hole is a hole. Thanks for that bon mot, Grandma! I'll never be whole, filling myself up constantly with these cream-puff people with no insides. I'm starving, imploding, dying. Perpetually malnourished. You were a twinkie, a diet twinkie, full of overheated aspartame, which polluted my body and soul, wasted my time, stole pieces of me, my precious time, and voraciously sucked the life out of me - while smiling and nodding innocently all the while. Do you think one could rip out one's navel with a wire hanger, dear reader? Perhaps, if it were well-made and sufficiently sharp. Perhaps the scientists are at work, at this very moment, shrinking wire hangers to the size of a few molecules - teaching them to self-replicate, and impale themselves by the thousands into the flesh of middle-aged narcissists.

A trick, a lie. I always come back to that. And I vowed never to be fooled again! Many times, in fact. Ephemera, all of you! Mindless, fleshy colonies of bacteria - projected on a scrim in a dark theater. I have a headache. Holy crap, there's half a wire hanger protruding from my skull! I must remember to post a note at the market - I am rather concerned that someone may have misplaced it, or shat it out - and is frantically looking for it. It may have been holding them upright for all I know, that and nothing else - it might have been their spine, their soul, their motivation to hold onto life for a few nanoseconds longer. I'm somewhat afraid to rip it out all at once. And yet I am curious, and half hungry for death, as I have always been, since I was a child - at some point my defenses will surely crumble.

What do you love? Whom do you love? (If anything or anyone.) You alluded to the sometimes empty quality of your marriage, your difficulty with your kids. And yet you are, at the end of the day, a clothes horse - nothing more. And quite full of horseshit, btw. That's too stupid to rise to the level of ironical. What matters to you? What matters to anyone? Who's going to give a fuck a hundred years from now? A hundred years, what a joke - six months after we're gone, who's going to do more than give us a passing thought? Do clouds and waves mourn? You'd better hope they do, narcissists. People are excrement. They consume everything around them in the most indiscriminate and disgusting manner - these bloated, heaving sacks of acid and fecal-filled guts, these worms, all dressed up with nowhere to go. For chrissakes, at least dress down, it would be a tad more honest.

So maybe I'll dream about you a few times, until you disappear into some half-lit cul-de-sac of dirt and rock, while the river roars by - obliterating everything - every memory, every trace of you. If we touched one another, it was from across a room - with thick vinyl gloves - fumbling, stupid and impotent. Then why do I want to squeeze my guts until they're blue, pull the wire hanger across my jugular until my paltry life-force spills onto the polyurethane floor, and scream at the impassive moon for allowing me to do this again?! Why does it not come tumbling out of the sky and crush me into dust?!

My life is a timed writing exercise. I've frightfully little to say, and the distinct and unfortunately appropriate impression that time is running out.

Goodbye. Well, there's an oxymoron for you.

Dear Dad

Dear Dad,

What's it like in heaven? I'll be generous, and assume that's where you are. Are people as empty and self-involved as ghosts or angels as they were here, in this gross, boorish neck of the universe's woods? Is it a relief? Is it torture? Can you see? Can you choose not to see? Do you choose not to?

How did we ever manage to envision a realm which is not full of all this sweaty, corporeal filth, these cutthroat genes, and blind amoral hunger? How did we dream up this ethereal, Platonic Idea, bullshit heaven? Just 'cuz we done thought it up don't mean it be. We done thought up plenty of dumb shit before that one, dat fer sure.

Why did you want to destroy Mommy? Did you not see how pathetic she was? Was there sufficient evil within her to override any of that, any of the more generous impulses you might otherwise have had? Did you not see how pathetic YOU were? How could you miss all that, Dad?

How is it that, as I write you this letter full of longing, rage, and utter mystification, I feel your presence so strongly? Is it just gene #427 on chromosome #19? Loneliness? Ambivalent grieving? Straightforward grieving? I am nothing - nothing other than this immense paramecium, lurching towards and away from appealing and dangerous stimuli. Slouching towards Bethlehem to hopefully not be born.

The only thing I can relate to is ideas. I think that might have been true of you, at least at one time, before you were ruined by Half-Moon News Distributors, and before you became a horrified and unwilling, or, at best, regretful and frustrated father.

Do you remember when you took me, as a kid, to Washington, D.C.? I barely do. Only that you were uncomfortable, to put it mildly. You didn't know what the fuck to do with me, or make of me. You tried, but failed. I love you for having tried. You didn't always try. You couldn't. You did that time.

Who were all those piece of shit women you spent the last fifteen years of your life with? Is not reason supposed to temper passion when you reach a certain age? And, if not reason, is not one's own valuation of one's self? One's dignity and self-respect? How could you not see who and what they were? You dated those God-awful JAP's just to piss off your dead mother? That served as adequate motivation? Holy crap, Dad.

I'm infected with your misogyny. I can see past it, at times - I CAN be empathic, but it dogs me, eats away at me. Kaley is an object of lust, or something vaguely resembling it, I suppose. But honestly, it's never fun with her, it's always a fucking chore - she always has this sad-sack face full of faux-seriousness and manufactured depth and passion when we're going at it. In truth, she's just a flawed person whom I have trouble seeing clearly, whom I'm constantly projecting onto, and with whom I think I've already fallen out of love. I'd ask you for advice here, but I'm afraid I'm almost certainly already following it. The real advice you gave me - THE WAY YOU LIVED YOUR FUCKING LIFE! I can only see people clearly once I've broken up with them anyway. Why did you jump from woman to woman? Actually, that question is of vanishingly little interest to me. Much more importantly - WHY THOSE WOMEN?!

Kaley thinks we become our best versions of ourselves when we die. Dear God - how shocking and stupid for a scientist to say such a thing. We're dying every minute. You're not that little boy in the pictures I looked at when I went through all your shit in the months and days after the funeral - you're not that adorable, dewy-eyed, young boy in that school uniform, that dude in the army. You molted. When you should have revolted. What an absolutely charming idea - little angel-boy Rickey Feltsman, in the prime of life, reading Yeats, Shakespeare, reading and talking about philosophy, and writing passionate love notes. I imagine your present-tense heaven is intravenous booze, a surfeit of ancient, yammering, hairy crone pussy, and oblivion - the latter, first and foremost. Although I may very well be projecting on that last count. Rest. Don't rest up for anything in particular - honestly, there isn't a helluva lot more that's going to be happening, that's left to do. Sleep dreamless sleep for all eternity. Schlaf gut und tief, mein geliebter Vater.

Is it true that Mommy was constantly threatening suicide? You were so disoriented and ranting by the time you started telling me shit like that. Were you fading in and out? Forgetting what your hooch-poisoned, wet-ass brain had said the day before? Did the testosterone shots make you want to hurt people, hurt her, lash out at everyone? Did you enjoy it when you did? Would you have been delighted, had I done it? Newsflash - I've done it. Many times. Are you beaming with paternal pride up there? While shitty harp music wafts through the clouds? That would be Hell, though, wouldn't it.

Selma has the IQ of a gerbil. I mean, she's not even stupid, she's pathetic - how she even walks around, on two legs, is some sort of deep, occult mystery. WHAT WAS THE DRAW? I suppose it must have felt good to be a hundred times smarter than the woman you were with - right, Dad? Did it make you feel secure, unchallenged, superior, worshipped? I suppose I kinda, sorta get it. At the same time that I find it despicable - pathetic.

You never condemned Molly, when she and I were locked in our ugly death throes - the horror show of those last months. That was big, noble, and wise of you. You could be big, noble, and wise. What happened? I sense the explanation right next to me, behind some fourth-dimensional scrim - I can almost reach out and touch it. But not quite.

You never learned to live alone. You left college, went right into the army, that safe, though deeply unpleasant, infantilizing womb, and then married. You're one of those guys in the statistics, who, after divorce, do much worse alone than the woman does. By the way, I want to formally thank you and Mommy for throwing me the fuck out of the house after Katy died. It was the best thing either of you ever did for me, even though you both did it out of pure selfishness. And, let's face it - it was SO soon after she died, that there was a healthy dose of sadism and cruelty involved, as well.

I remember you groggily staggering from the exam room to the office in that prick Dr. Kerpen's office, with blood oozing out of your gums and mouth, down your chin, and onto your shirt - disoriented, despondent, beaten. Who the fuck did that to you? He did. He killed you. Those testosterone shots killed you, I know it. I want him dead, that scumbag.

And who was the shrink before Green? Goodman? Ah yes - Goodman. And you were all wrapped up in some crazy, classic love/hate transference with him, too, unsurprisingly. And the shrink before that, the one to whom you sent the book "To an Early Grave ", when he was lying in intensive care? Innocently, as you thought and claimed to him at the time. Hahaha! "But the Times gave it a great review!" And there was one before that, too, no? I want never to walk through another therapist's door. It's revolving, revolting - a sticky spider's web of lies, manipulation, and greed - the walls dripping with poison, the floors toxic quicksand.

What is the big deal about sex, Dad? I'm forty-two, and I'm pretty much sick of it, over it. I'm disgusted by it, more often than not, not least by what a perverse trick it is, Nature's ultimate Ponzi scheme. Holy crap - the picture of your repulsive girlfriend, naked, that I found in your bedroom. It's enough to inspire auto-castration in the beholder. How could you lie next to that THING?!

I recall you looking out that ghastly window at the hospital. You could see the ambulances below. Did you ever think of jumping? I did.

I want to be inside your head when you ordered air guns from the Edge catalog. What the fuck were you thinking? That you'd put them on the mantlepiece? That you'd impress women with them? Selma told me that the glass part of the wall unit was your "trophy "display - full, as it was, of little piece-of-shit stuffed animals that various dinner whores had given you. Purchased at dollar stores, and intended to thank you for the thousands of dollars you had spent taking those porcine termagants to expensive Italian restaurants, where they stuffed their holes full of factory-farmed veal, while mulling over various and sundry other strategies they might employ to fleece you even further. Trophies, shooting, guns, phalluses, penis pumps, revenge.. Oy vey. Really??? I've almost got it, Dad - it's about to peek out from behind that fourth-dimensional scrim. I know it is. Nope, it's gone. It shall ever be thus. I will never understand.

It's late and I can't sleep. I should smoke some of your pot. A long time ago, you were friends with some young, hip girl, no? Chris or something? Didn't she smoke pot and wasn't she vaguely interesting? Unlike, ahem..., the rest of them? Maybe not - maybe she just had big tits.

And the eighty-seven "vitamins" on the Lazy Susan - what the fuck was that all about? BEE POLLEN? For chrissake, Dad. Self-hypnosis tapes? The disciple of Yeats and Shakespeare was now bending the knee to Tony Robbins? Jesus, you were miserable. Way back then, too. The Yeats-reading Dad, the Half-Moon News vice-president Dad, the bee pollen, JAP-fucking Dad - all miserable.

So now I've had two hits of your pot. But I just feel stupid - weird in my body, and vaguely paranoid. What was the draw there? I get it - at twenty years-old - I get the obsession with fucking, too, but what was the draw, in your late sixties? Wasn't it time to make an attempt at being even slightly dignified? To spurn the vulgar, embrace the noble? Just a teeny-weeny bit? To not say to your son, "Now that I can't drink and fuck, I'm ready to die"? Lovely, Dad. I dunno - now you've got all of eternity to be blank, to be dead, to be gone. You're gone now. You could've been a little more "here" while you were here. There ya go - my little nod to Gertrude Stein.

Why am I even writing this?

Love,

Your confused son, who wishes he could talk to you,

and misses you terribly

Excerpt from the
Gobbledygook Book of Revelations

There's something ghastly at the edge of town - a dust cloud, a whispering from the sanatorium, a clean slate, an apple cart, upset and preset from the outset. A reason men hold their breaths and staple their dicks to their abdomens, wag their tongues, and stare at the sun till their retinas bleed.

There's mange on my soul, bloody, pulpy hemorrhoids on my heart, cellulite on my eyelids, and scorpions in my temples. There are scorpions in all the temples - the rabbis have discarded us all, thrown us to the wolves, along with common sense and all vestiges of humanity, then buried themselves in the chill of the desert night, headfirst, their rectums beaten down by sandstorms, their minds consumed by hallucinations, and their entrails gorged upon by vultures.

How did I get in this body? I didn't ask for it. And I certainly didn't ask for it to decay, once I received it. I didn't ask for this knowledge. Take it from me - drown me in oblivion, in Morpheus, the underworld, the undertow... Park at your own risk. The ticking of this goddamned wristwatch is deafening. And, by the way - keep close watch on one's wrists - they are veiny and tender, full of nerves, eager to touch and be touched, and deathly afraid of being severed. Severe weather is forecast, whether you like it or not. It's coming - the paths and roads slick, treacherous, enticing, comical, heartless, and embalmed.

Who has done this thing? Who has brought me here, who has dredged me up, kicking and weeping and pissing and screaming, from the blind primordial sludge, where all is forgetting? There will be a solar eclipse, there will be bloodcurdling cries, and sacrifices - the moon will not remove itself from between the sun and earth without a struggle, without the blood of a half-million Iraqi women and children being spilled into a Walmart teacup, and ten thousand choking dolphins beaching themselves on the shores of Staten Island - while the smokestacks belch black filth, and the old nuclear facility begins to break apart. William Carlos Williams was a bit of a pollyanna. Carlos Santana is in the green room, eating a banana. King Arthur is busy banging his sister, Morgana.

I saw the best minds of my generation believe their own stories, their own lies, their own music. I saw every last Platonic ideal in art, in literature, reduced to a miserable, godforsaken brain structure, chemical excrement from a dying star. I saw the seven-headed beast of Babylon slouching towards Bethlehem, with Kathie Lee Gifford at the reins. I saw Esau, what an eyesore I saw. I'm sorely tempted, surly, at best, and, most probably, according to my grandmother at least, Shirley.

If you've read this far, you already know how many letters Manny Goldberg has sent out to unsuspecting charitable organizations. And if you know that, all is not lost. At least Bill Clinton, despicable as he is, married Hillary, despicable as she is - at least she has some semblance of an evil, Machiavellian brain. As compared with the creature JFK married - a pampered, anorexic clothes horse, destined and happy to break Maria Callas' heart. If I could pull what I am out from the demolition-derby site of my childhood, and offer it, somehow, to others, to the world, I would. But I can't, so I won't. I will, instead, contemplate my beloved naval Academy. I will classify myself 4F, and drink deeply of the bitter draught that blows through my guts and eats them alive. I will render myself to the best of my abilities, such as they are, and wish that they were very different. I will tell myself that whatever culture survives a millennium from now, if any survives at all, won't give a crap about Wagner, or Schopenhauer, or Einstein, other than as a few quaint footnotes and stepping-stones in rarely read textbooks. I will go gently into that good night. Good night.

As grains of sand in the sour gas, these are the days of our lives - spent in the daze of our collective lies, and displayed on the dais on which our lice and maggot- infested souls will be inspected by St. Peter, spat upon, and marked "return to sender".

Fondest of illusions

It's springtime in the park, but there's a frost upon my soul,
Which has me every morning in its grip -
As a student of anxiety, who's on full scholarship,
I never get it under my control.

Why phantoms rip me from my sleep, and what it is they crave,
Is something they insist remain unknown -
I only know that I'm into a raging whirlwind thrown,
From which I'm often dropped into a cave

That's swarming with the spirits of the dead and of the living,
Who don't make their intentions very clear -
I've no idea the reason that both they and I are here,
Or whether they'll be kind or unforgiving.

Sometimes I'll bolt upright, in the hopes that I'll recover
From this hypnagogic madness and confusion -
But sometimes I embrace it, whether real or illusion -
For what if I encounter an old lover

Who comforts me with evidence that, when it's time to die,
That which is to come will make amends
For all that I've endured, which she clearly comprehends?
But what if she's some sort of Lorelei

Enticing me to drown, or dash my brains out on a reef,
To sound my dark and much-disguised death knell,
To throw me off a cliff, into the boundless depths of Hell,
And pains from which they'll never be relief?

That's possible, I guess, but when I look into her eyes,
A calm upon me suddenly descends -
We weren't only lovers - we were deep and lifelong friends,
With all the faith and trust which that implies.

I hold her to my breast and make an oath not to upset her -
She loved me then, and seems to love me now -
I tell her that I'll follow her, and make a solemn vow
That if we're parted, I will come and get her

Whether here on Earth, or in this cryptic afterlife -
Whether she's a product of my dreams,
Or lies here in my arms, and is exactly what she seems -
My once upon a time and future wife.

My existence is a crapshoot - it's amoral and unfair -
To face another day, I must believe
That, after all I've gone through, I'll be given a reprieve -
But truth to tell, that's all up in the air.

I slog through life, not knowing why it is I suffer so -
Perhaps, in some past life, there were some crimes
Of which I cannot know, and which are drowned by midnight's
chimes,
Which don't make clear what I'm to undergo

Whether here on Earth, or in some small, or great beyond,
Wrapped in Cathy's arms or all alone -
Whether I'll be blissful or face terrors yet unknown,
Or how to either one I might respond.

I've become accustomed to the arrows and the slings
Of fortunes spent in landfills and debris -
Yet even though it's risible, I still aspire to be
That person for whom hope eternal springs.

And hence, I now believe, that since I've paid this heavy price,
There'll come a time when I am with my wife in Paradise.

Form happens

Form happens
To give sadness substance.
In its fast-folding shroud,
The unseen decays and withers,
Fugitive desires of the heart's twilit hours.

Time happens
To take form's contours,
Ushering the weary flesh
Through portals flecked with wondrous, spinning light.

Now the talk is all of parallel universes -
Of endless splits,
Collisions -
Of perhaps-visitations
Of molten hungry seas,
Thrice-blessed and amber-lit
By moons of youth,
Lust,
And destiny,
In galaxies like this one -
Where all is,
Has ever been,
And always will be
Permitted -
And where each and every being and thing
Has been countless times
Reveled in,
Railed against,
Embraced,
Suffered,
Scorned,
Feared, forgiven, forgotten...
And reborn.

Four poems

I.

Sunlight sprays particles of mist,
Which invigorate some -
But serve to remind others
That this life coursing through our veins
Is a tremulous thing,
Which can leave a robin full-throated,
Or unable to sing
To the babes in its nest,
Who are crying for love -
For something quite other
Than worms from above
Their parched mouths and damp feathers,
Which will thrive, or perish, depending on whether
The whims of the world
And the heart of the mother
Conspire to let these poor creatures discover
Their wings, and fly
Towards ambivalent sunlight -
The dawns of forgetting,
And the dusks of regretting
The unbearable days they enclose.

Thrown into life
By an unconscious power,
Which spews and which wretches
Each minute and hour
To call forth a slug, or a man, or a flower.

Those who cower in the crevices of folded wings,
Waiting for the fearsome storm to abate,
Pour out their dreams and their terrors, and things
God couldn't possibly have meant to create.

44

Through a windowsill, the tired flower stretches
Its neck towards a lonely sparrow
Hovering above its nest
In great waves of sorrow -
Seduced by the sunlight, that treacherous traitor,
Who promised us life -
But sooner or later
We saw what was there,
When she lit up the sky
With her promises of youth, and the breathtaking lie
That we were immortal.

But perhaps we are...

The dust of a giant and nebulous star,
That floats in the ether
And one day emerges
As a slug, or a flower, or simply the urges
To bask in the sunlight
And choose not to mourn
Our transient destiny -
Immortal, unborn.

Sleep now, my precious, beloved friend -
For tomorrow
You must dance in the sun -
While the universe echoes to your laughter
For an instant,
And then
Is done.

II.

In the country of dreams, time does not exist -
Young men's teeth crumble,
And old men fret about exams missed -
There is death, and youth, and mornings kissed
By sunlight, filtered through the scrim
Of memory, hope, and the curious whim
Of the dreamer,
Who floats above the ground with wings -
Unaware, until aloft,
Without a sound,
Surveying grass and tree -
And now, amazed -
Aghast that he is free
From care, from pain, from bodily woes,
From the slings and arrows shot by those
Who never loved him -
Those who've died,
Who made him grieve,
Who made him cry
Tears of blood, and shattered faith -
Tears addressed to stone-deaf wraiths,
Who can't appear in dreams, because
The innocence of sleep
Is swaddled in a church, which was
Never defiled with the filth of age,
Decrepitude, senescence, rage
Over milk spilt by a boy, who dreamt
Of innocent flight, which seemed
To bathe his senses in a numinous glow,
Which touched him now as if, as though
He'd always been alive and new,
And sprouted fresh, and green - and through
Years in which waking life had seemed
Impassable, entombed, unredeemed.

He soars now free above the clouds,
Which once were black with dust and shrouds
Of hooded figures, cloaked in darkness -
Lurching, clutching,
But now with far less
Power to stab,
With a blood-red knife,
His dreams of freedom
From specters and ghosts,
And from his need
To be near them,
To be like them
In his waking life.

Those who once chased him
Through chasms and tunnels,
Rife with sideshows of flesh -
Through poison-drenched funnels,
Boiling over with venom and hate -
They're too late!
He's asleep now -
Enveloped in dreams,
Where nothing can touch him
Except that which seems
Tender, and gentle, and blissful, and kind -
Unburdened by the tricks and the vagaries
Of his heretofore unfortunate life,
And his once
Deeply clouded
Mind.

III. Pathetic

"Pathetic"
Is a word
That was once imbued
With nobility,
But now is but a crude
Gesture of contempt
For those whose puny lives
Are bent
Into twisted shapes -
Unnatural things,
Ground beneath the feet of kings.

Gentlemen don't deign to recognize
Destinies of such paltry size...

Behold the tragic mighty oak,
Alongside the cruel and cosmic joke -
Both lashed by furies
For being born -
The first with praise,
The latter scorn.

What constitutes the difference?
Say!
The actor's gifts?
The role, the play?
The audience's digestive systems?
The age itself? Its customs, wisdom?

One knows the difference without thinking -
One is simply not worth sinking
Low enough to contemplate,
While the other pursues a loftier fate,
Ennobled in tragedies and fiction,
And sanitized with flowery diction.

It's only the naked brute perception,
The stuff of mayhem and deception,
Which separates the crone with cancer
From that illustrious scarf-slain dancer,
Who is now the stuff of stage and screen,
While that wretched woman is never seen -
Her memory but dying embers
In the minds of a few sad family members.

Her end was grievous, painful, dark -
But her life's impression will barely spark
The leaves
Which will turn,
And fall,
And scatter -
And more than likely
Will not matter
In a day,
Or two,
A week,
A year...

Which one are you, my love, my dear?
The grandiose and noble hero?
A Bonaparte? An Emperor Nero?
Or the purely existential zero?

IV.

The enervating thoughts
That cloud my days and soul
Struggle to be born
Through the muffled gurgling
Of the suffocated sea floor
Hissing sinister up my spine -
I stand alone -
Unnerved,
Undone by ships
Of venomous pirates
Taking harbor
In a soft and pulpy mass
Of flesh,
Once vibrant and singing,
Like a laser
Through time and space -
For an instant,
Through all eternity...

There was a time
I threw myself,
Thin and garrulous,
Over fences, lightly
Dancing through youth
With flexed heartstrings, and eyes hungry
For the jugular of life -
For the warmth of apple-rosy breasts
Pushed close
To my lean and wolfish body -
The price I'm now paying,
Crouched, withered, and alone,
As the sad moon weeps and falls from the sky,
And the sun begets another idiot spring
Sprouting tendrils of lunatic virginity
Through an eternally naive
And now once again blushing earth -

Green and strong with the sap of youth,
Limbs bursting, and bustling with fists that force
Their way through to the extraordinarily lazy,
And seemingly endless
Afternoon of life.

But now I sit,
Still -
Startled by the setting sun,
The dusk,
The hoary harbinger of frigid night -
Believing only that what was
Must surely continue
To be, or if not to be,
Then to warm
Disconsolate, frosty veins,
Which once held a roaring river,
Now muted
To a dank and dreary dribble.

Memories are sweet,
And sometimes sufficient
To quiet rumbling,
Disaffected passions
With romantic notions
Of what my life has meant to others.

But in the dead of night,
The regrets, the faintly gnawing hunger, the horror
That when those who once knew me are gone,
It will be
As if I had never been.

Unless I somehow ripple
Through all eternity -
Taken up in luminous wings,
And swaddled in the warm embrace
Of God's loving gaze.

Goodnight, and may God bless

God bless Mom, and God bless Dad,
Though it's others I wish I had had -
But God does not bless angry cranks,
So I've let go and now give thanks
For all the good things in my life -
God bless my partner, friend, and wife,
God bless the innocent and mild,
God bless my sweet, angelic child,
God bless my Labrador Retriever,
And me, the wannabe believer.

As days and telomeres grow short,
You lose your spark, you lose your court,
But newfound mercy's a reminder
That though grown dumber, you've grown kinder -
Sans your frantic zest for living,
You're more thoughtful and more giving -
As bodies age and life gets tougher,
You feel it more when others suffer -
You pick their burden up, and carry it
Away on a celestial chariot,
Drawn through milky skies above
On axes, now grown bold as love.

Each thing happened as it had to,
All the things I wasn't glad to
Bear now stand revealed as just
Forgotten dreams and fairy dust -
I see it in the setting sun,
God has blessed us, every one -
And when things grow all grey and dim,
They'll still make sense, at least to Him.

Farewell to all that I once knew -
God bless me, and God bless you.

Hello, I must be going...

The perpetual anxiety of a great horned owl, squeezed into a can of sardines -

The bandwidth of a junked computer, swallowed in a landfill -

The once killer whale guts, full of plastic - choking on oil slicks and looking for its mate, long since dragged off in a net, and devoured by hungry Chinese peasants, on a black beach, under a sweaty, blood-red sun -

Welcome to the Hotel Chernobyl - where Mom and Dad cough you up out of ancient phlegm onto a leaking rowboat sinking into an Amazonian river, where you're sniffed by blind anacondas and surrounded by wannabe academic alligators wearing pince-nez glasses reading Emily Dickinson to burnt-out adventure-seekers clutching their extremities, recently stitched together by doctors operating out of swine-infested barns frequented by overfed urban vegans and formerly Tasmanian, though presently Appalachian, devils, for the moment out for lunch in a mad frenzy of honor killings - in which pregnant worms hold seances for dead ancestors, lit by gothic candelabras with sharp-razored edges, gutting intestines and squeezing vagal nerves till hearts burst in terror - pounding, pounding, pounding - drowning the shrieks of trains in the distance carrying fat businessmen with sleep apnea home to their resentful dwarfish wives with brains bursting full of cable-news lies and cat-borne parasites -

Rain drenching the rat-park through which breeders wheel carriages full of newly sentient filth, shaking rattles made by slaves in underground caves, whipped and scourged by Nibelungen despots howling, howling, howling with glee, waiting for dead suns to suck the earth dry and pulling acid rains from over-fertilized lawns to the accompaniment of insane leaf-blowing madmen back to the weeping clouds above - dripping mucusy tears into deranged, sap-filled oaks, all the while waiting, waiting, waiting to die - and for the blessed sound of chainsaws - the promise of relief from fingers sawed off and sucked up into 6000 horsepower wood chippers operated by lunatics newly

escaped from private prisons run by bankers living in plastic
mansions sitting on plastic lawns and drinking water bottled from
toxic sludge and immediately re-marketed by brutal Filipino
dictators ordering the deaths of reality-show contestants, who
had only just now been proclaiming store-bought love in hovels
entered through tunnels opening on campuses of private
universities with endowments composed of junk-bonds slapped
together by defense contractors, fast-food franchises, and run by
transhumanist hobbits busy popping dangerous, overpriced
supplements sold on the dark web by wannabe Columbine-killers
living in Upper East Side trailers parked by burnt-out strip joints,
where the unemployed girls linger, syringes hanging from
withered arms dripping with jism and the longing for Pocono
weekends with rail thin pimps wearing oversized hats and driving
forty-year-old yellow Cadillacs made in plants by disgruntled
knife-wielding postal workers with posters of Adam Lanza
adorning their roadside dumpsters -

You there - busy unwinding in the world you pollute with
your blindness and factory-farmed-filled bellies, overdosing on
porcine antibiotics and flat screen T.V.'s playing old Hitchcock
movies, free with endless ads for psycho-pharmaceutical poisons,
on stations run by bloated CEO's wearing polka-dot bowties
licked clean by hairless trophy wives in germ-proof bubbles
situated on seas of stolen penguin eggs collected by morbid
documentary filmmakers speaking in borrowed accents created
by speech pathologists on Hollywood movie sets run by chest-
thumping orangutans screaming bloody fucking murder at
mousy attendants with heart conditions treated by money-
hungry cardiologists in run-down clinics underwritten by tax
dollars paid by bearded buffoons living in broken trailers just
above the poverty line, and just below the normative IQ of
atypically hateful murders of warmongering crows engaged in
bloody guerrilla warfare conducted in dense forests about to
burst into global-warming-induced flames -

Pain is the stuff of life - graduating to boredom-drenched
commodes, when given permission by dirty fuzz-buckets in blue,
wielding penis-shaped nightsticks borrowed from angry, sex-
deprived wives fearing for their lives, whose very own little blue

devil is just now driving his twelve-year-old, grease-sputtering Chevrolet onto curbs full of the piss of poodles walked by fat ladies hurrying to luncheons at two-bit diners in suburban hells populated by barely-conscious bags of wrinkled flesh, and long-winded gasbags serving slimy grilled cheese sandwiches to bloated firemen in red suspenders and mute camel drivers watching stock prices on screens suspended from spider-infested ceilings by duct tape made in Sao Paolo by Brazilian women, whose skins fester with boils and cancers which drive their men into the hands of arms-trafficking cops and Andalusian robber barons -

I used to blame it on the Bossa Nova, but have recently learned lessons of a very different nature taught by Porsche-driving minimalist composers writing clueless commissions offered by tone-deaf hedge-fund managers suffering from undiagnosed brain bleeds -

Goodbye, Norma Jean, Diana, Anna Nicole Smith - the tabloids will never be the same, filled as they are with rotting vegetables wrapped in wax paper stolen from fish markets operating in the bowels of purported libraries on Main Streets of every small American hellhole-town, where crumbling sheetrock walls fall in between the legs of Korean masseuses - smirking, smirking, smirking - as they rifle through pockets of dry-cleaned XXXL K-mart chinos hanging in yards of deathless disciples turned upside-down, and suspended by ropes from wheels of metallic teeth cribbed from Marquis de Sade novels, and cancelled by evangelical husbands cheating on their Tammy Faye wives with mustached prostitutes in ne'er-attended airport toilets.

And Goodbye, Yellow Brick Roads - danced upon by amphetamine-injecting child actors smoking extra-long cigarettes on abandoned sets frequented by famished foxes and hysterical hyenas, driven brutally from natural habitats ruined by developers with slot machines and heart-shaped bathtubs, where there should, by rights, have been only faces of DEATH, DEATH, DEATH - coughing up palpitations and reading lines from teleprompters full of lines composed by incompetent underpaid writers which nevertheless manage to effectively convey their soul-crushing reminders of mortality -

Why should tonight be different from any other night? I've forgotten the other three freaking questions. But the answer? The answer, my friend, is blowing smoke up the asshole of the miscreants who rolled the dice which pulled you from the ether and consigned you to this Hell.

Hidden Gift Tax

The fucking Long Island Railroad. It's drizzling, and the train is a half-hour late. Look at this despicable jerk. I want to throw this smirky-ass, mustached, beret-wearing fuck-tard headfirst on the tracks, and kick his tobacco-yellow teeth in bloody, if he tries to hoist himself up to safety, so he is once again splayed out the tracks like some Aztec sacrificial offering - until the train roars in and rips him in half. I want to watch, and gloat, while his rubbery, Looney Tunes-like, blood-writhing stumps of legs kick wildly from their severed spinal cord, mindlessly, violently, hopelessly - his petrified eyes imploring someone, anyone, me, God, his Mommy, as they glaze over in the stupefied horror, betrayal, and absurdity of this eternal moment. I want to keep my cool, uncaring, voyeur-of-the-universe eyes riveted, as the guts ooze out of his body cavity - slowly, hesitantly, like science-fiction alien, deep-sea creatures ripped from their familiar, volcanic vent homes on the ocean floor, which are thrown violently onto a slab of concrete - to sputter, wriggle, grow brittle, and die.

The train passed only seconds ago, and already the pigeons and crows have come to roost - to dine, to swallow, to digest, and doubtless later defecate, his apparently delicious, mucous-y eye blobs, in some blighted, urban, wannabe but not really forest, violated with telephone poles, and the arid, meaningless noise of the sordid, greasy suburbs. Eyes are something of a delicacy, then, although perhaps only for the airborne. One wonders about the hors d'oeuvres preferences of rats and earthworms, who are also sure to arrive not long from now.

This marvelous ability I seem to possess. Is it real? It feels as if it is. I've frozen all the onlookers into a state of perpetual, preconscious befuddlement, timeless and moronic, like that cheesy, imbecilic, third-rate novelist who freezes time just so he can cop a feel. Stop the march of time to look up a whore's dress, will you? You pathetic, little, baby-carrot dick-driven loser coward. There is a universe of pain, violence, oozing decay, of garishly lit panoramas of creatures eating creatures, busy being eaten themselves, all under a blind, and utterly apathetic, mediocre, middle-aged star, in some quadrant of a supremely humdrum galaxy, a star which will burn your eyeballs into charred, smoking stumps of barbecued silly-putty if you look at it too long, and which lights up the nightmare of others' and of your own ongoing daily decay, when you have the misfortune to look anywhere else.

So there they stand - the fools, the automatons, the mindless breeders - the stroller-pushing hags, with their pot-bellied, hockey-fan husbands, mannequins with backwards baseball caps, all with the vague intuitions that life is a ghoulish joke, hovering protectively and proudly over their little, sheep-blond, Hitler-youth, crewcut, video-gaming, zombie children vermin.

I'm unsure of my powers. Were I to kick any of them onto the tracks, would they plummet back into the mists and streams of time? Plunge forwards to the moment of their demise? To their likely sojourn in hell when the time comes? Could I do this thing? Do I have the nerve? I haven't tried it - yet. Would they not wake up, screaming, begging for mercy, as if they had blinked for a moment, and suddenly awoke face-to-face with Satan, amidst endless eternal flames and deafening shrieks for mercy? One would hope so.

Jesus said, "Love thine Enemy." Now that the new millennium is upon us, that adage sounds a bit dated and sentimental, don't you agree, oh my charred, bone-weary, and broken readers? Let's rework it a bit. I think I'd rather torture, mutilate, and disembowel out of pure, unmitigated hatred, but hardly restrict it to them - better still? - someone I love, or could love, who looks primordially appealing to me, as well. Yes, this will be my particular, self-prescribed, self-help regimen. I'm convinced this is to be my own particular road less traveled. Wayne Dyer meets the Antichrist. I'll overcome myself - Nietzsche would approve.

There, near the waiting room, a little, red-haired girl - innocent, dressed like a Brontë character, porcelain-pure, divine, with her gently glowing hippie mommy. Do I have the nerve? I look over the cliff's edge into the black abyss of the future, of my soul, of freedom.

58

I consider kicking an old woman onto the tracks. One of those ancient fuckers that might as well be hot-iron, forehead-branded, "I'm just a mean young cunt who was perversely lucky enough to have grown old." You know the type. But it won't be satisfying. She'd barely know what's about to happen. I suppose the carnage would be appealing in some sort of clinical way, and the screams would be some sort of new music I haven't yet heard (I imagine they always are), but what sort of thrill would this be? That insipid, phony-ass, B.B. King, not really blues tune starts ringing in my buzzing, sleep-deprived mind's ear.

Straw dog, paper tiger, fall guy. I must kill what I love to be free.

I consider violently elbowing a particularly ugly, fat hausfrau to the ground, and kicking her polyester, Tommy Hilfiger ass over the landing. Only - dear God, I would have to endure that voice! I'd be unable to wait for the train to finish her off - I'd be forced to jump down on the tracks, and stomp her head in myself. It would likely feel delicious, the warm goo of her brain on my shoe, the stringy cartilage of her nose hanging like flower tendrils over the bright steel of the hot, moonlit track. The body lives on for minutes and minutes, it is said. And the stupider they are, the longer they take to die, one imagines - the longer they pointlessly cling to life, like insects drowning in a squalid public restroom. I would take notes. Information like this could prove very useful to someone.

How about kicking that filthy, wannabe bodybuilder/narcissist over the side? This is getting old, has become a bore. Ninety-seven channels, with nothing on.

There, the Spanish guy who thought he was so tough, who was trying to stare me down right before I froze everyone - there, the beefy Islanders fan, the gangly, pimply-faced kid with the Metallica t-shirt, the overcompensating bitch-on-wheels businesswoman with the briefcase, with the hard-looking face, and black, dried-out roots. I am a tired immortal, doomed to an endlessly insipid, solitary board game.

But now it's just the two of them I see, frozen-standing - the little, porcelain, red-haired angel, and her honey-sweet mom.

Kill what you love, and you'll be free. Free! Kill what you love.

Would it count if I did it quickly, and they didn't suffer? Could I still claim to be Zarathustra on the mountaintop, or would I, instead, be a sniveling, spineless, laughably apologetic "assisted-dying" enabler, a sort of Florence Henderson meets Jack Kevorkian?

They must suffer, and I must hear their screams reverberate up to heaven and back again, and not answer them. There is no other way.

Do it and I will be free - me, Icarus, though with melt-proof wings, singed and purified by fire - a blissfully disconnected, observing consciousness, plugged in to the spine-tingling beauty, color, and sound of the now clearly dreamed universe. No nooses around my neck, no Isadora scarves hanging spoke-ready, no albatrosses, or weights of the world, no Achilles' heels - burned, hardened, alabaster, with eyes and ears drunk-ful of ecstatic, sensuous perfume and music. No heart.

I approach the little girl. I kneel. I look into her tiny, wide eyes - naive, fearless, puppy-pure, ready. Are these my tears or is my flesh melting? If I killed all the others, but left these two - who would know, who would be the wiser?

A bloated, hag-witch, whom I had imagined eviscerating moments ago, now murmurs a laughably faint, Christian prayer from just below me, hanging on to life by a cockroach-blind thread.

My brain screams - shut up, shut up, shut up!!! I jump over the landing, grab her by the throat, pick up her head, and stare soul-deep into her eyes. Look at me, witch, look at me and die. Carry my memory-picture encoded in your idiot neurons, right up to the throne of your despicable God. Convey to him my supreme contempt, my loathing for all he has created - this vile, spinning orb of shit, this terrestrial hell of striving virus creatures, shredding each other to bits, hanging on just long enough to shoot their little salmon-jism into the ongoing flood of madness and slaughter.

In my mind, I hoist myself back on the platform to her, to them. Look at me, my daughter, my sister, my lover, my life.

Tell me how to kill you, to shut down my own reflexes, to sever every last connection with the living, and with hope. Teach me how to do it, as you taught me long ago to need, to hunger, to languish, to be afraid, to be alone, plate-glass-bubble encased and alone. Undo the spell, I beg you.

You are a lie. There are worms from the future crawling out of the sides of your eyeballs, little angel girl - your tongue is a hungry serpent, and your smile is Satan's sleight of hand. You transmigrate from youth to youth, damning and tempting me with your fishhook mouth, and your false claims of love and eternity. This child is merely a wax puppet, a piece of cloth a demon wears and discards at the first signs of decay, and, oh, but how quickly they appear - in the first rosy blush of spring they lie, waiting, with their fatal gifts of madness and deceit.

My face is hot, burning hot. My joints are rat-trap cold and taut.

I cannot do it. Any of it. I cannot. Instead, I retrieve the severed limbs and scattered organs, one by one, from below, the detritus and blood-seed of life. I pile them high around the two goddesses, whose gaze lacerates me, that gaze which terrifies me more than anything else, and from which I have always attempted to flee. And yet the stench is meat-sweet and soothing. I toss a match into the pulpy, viscous eye-jelly by my left foot. The flames engulf everything - the dead, the platform, my clothes, myself, everything but these two visions of unearthly beauty - these harpies in angels' garb - the very sight of them warms me, thrills me, delights me - and is, all the while, a poisonous harpoon in my guts. They rise like celestial Mona Lisas, while all around us all there is only searing, cooking flesh, the cries of the agitated, hungry, swarming birds who circle overhead, and the sounds of the beams beneath our feet, burning and breaking. This is all I can cough up? This will stand as my own personal, chickenshit Götterdämmerung? It's not even an 8mm movie Fellini made and discarded, with an embarrassed shudder, as a twelve year-old.

Who writes these words?

He who falls endlessly through an infinite well of loss and dashed hopes, as the faintly glowing skylight grows more and more hidden and distant. He who cannot live, could never live, and now cannot die.

The trains pass me now, on both sides, and with increasing frequency. I see the distant faces, an endless parallel universe of Eleanor Rigbys, who never see me, who simply stare blankly ahead at their empty, cyclical destiny, their eternal, unwanted return - as inaccessible as the tomb of Cleopatra to such as I, who lives outside of time, space, and the sordid tendrils of love, which I desperately crave, and from which I frantically flee.

I understand, Daddy. The horror at the end of the world, at the base of my spine - the horror you saw so clearly, but couldn't stare down, and from which you could not run. Come to me tonight, in dream - slit my throat from the inside out, catch my soul in a paper bag and drag it down to hell, on a Greyhound bus full of mental patients, reeking of piss, sweat, stale cigarettes, and mothballs. Scatter it underneath a black tar pit where it can squirm, sightless, with its self cast off in rivers of sweet forgetting…

I am now the hostage of the Gnostic Demiurge

When moods like this o'ertake me, I can neither see nor feel -
My blood turns black and clots, and my extremities congeal -
The world I knew just yesterday is now no longer real -
It feels as if there'll never be an end to this ordeal.

All who end up here abandon all hope of salvation -
This inferno of anxiety, and frozen agitation,
Cognitive impairment, psychomotor retardation,
Misanthropic misery, and cruel self-flagellation.

Someone who has never been afflicted by depression
Can only have a simple, one-dimensional impression
Of what I am enduring, its inception and progression -
All they see's a face devoid of affect and expression.

For what was me has now from both my flesh and blood been
torn,
And stands before what lingers on, dejected and forlorn -
What's left is barely human, and for things one does not mourn -
If only I had had the luck to never have been born.

When I am not this ill, I have no real inkling why
I fall into these snake pits, where I only wish to die -
The world remains quite nonchalant, it simply passes by,
And were I of a mind to ask Him, God would not reply.

So count your blessings, you that walk the Earth without a care -
Be thankful you're not suffocating, gasping for some air,
Buried under Himalayan mountains of despair,
While no one gives a rat's ass, insofar as you're aware.

There's nothing you can do, there is no way you can prepare -
No vitamin, no lover - neither macho pose nor prayer
Can guarantee you'll never be entangled in its snare -
This loathsome beast can find you anytime and anywhere.

I cover the waterfront

I cover the waterfront,
Only to discover
Dehydrated quarterbacks,
Punting silver dollars
Over spectacled traders' laptops -
Dancing under half-moons
With dirt-poor vagrants,
Whose unsoiled buttocks
Tick existential made-in-China minutes
Off nine-lived cats,
Scratching collars
And posting goals -
Meanwhile
Sweat-drenched boys
Sleep fitfully -
Too tired
To remain awake
For three-part dirges
Composed of four-bar phrases,
And performed by
Quintessentially sex-crazed septets -
Tapped over dead phone lines
To doddering spinsters,
Nursed by ill-advised wheelers, dealers, and pricks,
Looming over credit cards
Forged in valleys
Of aboriginal gloaming
And once-gleaming pennies
Long ago impounded -
Laying dormant
In faraway moused porticos,
Where the steady state
Of pinochle games,
Played by Fred Hoyle impersonators,
Served foot-long sandwiches,
Predigested and vomited

Into ancient yunomis
by Bill Cosby acolytes
Bearing Betamax tapes,
Soaked in lemon juice
And sprayed with Pledge,
In holy rites
Performed by pedophile priests
In underground charnel houses,
Is interrupted only
By leprous waitresses
Seeking monumental gratuities -
Bearing trays
Filled with a seemingly inexhaustible supply
Of rancid Oreos -
Their enormous breasts
Barely contained
In Uncle Ruckus t-shirts,
Poached from Mole People
Living in dark subway tunnels,
Where the vision thing
Is in short supply.

Look to your betters -
Before your ambivalence
Sours into a putrid landfill,
Signed, sealed, and canceled
In a psychotic stampede
Of midnight postal services
Danced on freshly waxed floors -
Candlelit by grinning mohels,
Whipping nervous mohelets,
Bearing gritted dentures,
In rutted soap dishes,
To petrified, unemployed woodsmen -
Patrolled by coked-up, Wittgenstein-ian, doctoral students,
Locked down in prisons
Of maximum cerebral insecurity,

Where crews of uncivil, horned owls
Chase stuttering vermin
Up the Mount of All Lives,
Where Jesus lies
His weary bones
On ancient Astro turf -
Salvaged,
Sandwiched,
And purged
By dice-wielding Furies,
Giving sermons
And bearing vinegar
To ghoulish, parched, and puckered lips
Hungry for the kiss of life -
The pride of death,
Stuffed sidelong
In a corrugated box
Standing tall
In a musty Office Depot warehouse,
Between petty thieves
Whistling leitmotifs
From Act One Siegfried
To blackbirds and ravens
In the dead of night.

But you must look to the dawn
For your son, Ma,
Mother,
Fucker -
What they've done to your song
While you lay bleeding -
It's alright -
'Tis not the moment
To be busy dying -
Now is the moment
You must learn to fly.

If it is true

<Depression is, in part, an inflammatory disorder... Research suggests that inhaling Mycobacterium vaccae can help illicit a less depressed state of mind. (You can get a dose just by taking a walk in the wild, or rooting around in the garden.) By triggering the production of immune cells that curb the inflammatory reaction typical of allergies, Mycobacterium vaccae may help ease the inflammatory reaction, and hence reduce said depression. >

If it is true that sniffing dirt reduces depression,
Then eating worms surely promises salvation -
To leap again over fences, in one's lean and wolfish twenty-six-
year-old body -
To live, as if no one had ever ripped your heart out from its
shoddy casing,
And violently thrown it fifty floors to the ground out of a drug-
infested housing project window...

Time grows like an army of enormous, carnivorous weeds,
encircling fragile hothouses
In which prostitutes lollygag on imported park benches
Discussing the Ding an sich -
As their flesh sags in a frenzied orgy of cellulite,
The implications are lost on them -
Like Kurvenal, fussing over his bleeding master,
The gravity of the situation eludes them,
Situated and subject, as it is, to gravity -
The steady pull of a hungry, iron core
Dreaming of its Cesarean birth in a belching star.

Major Tom and Diver Dan search valiantly for answers in
extinct marine life,
Deceiving oysters with freshly-built crucifixes on pockmarked
moons -
The virulent contagion of various vascular diseases in the
confusion of the assembled vessels
(Or vassals, as noted by Hagen - Act II, Götterdämmerung)

Has baffled the medical establishment since Galen roamed the
Roman Forum,
Since hunters and gathers conversed with tree-borne snakes,
And applied their endless leeches to wannabe spotted owls in the
dense forests of prehistoric Europe -
Find your coat and grab your hat, shuffle off towards home plate
and kick up a little dust for your adoring fans -
The crowd roars,
The ashes scatter
(The comedy is rerun on pay-per-view)
As Mick Jagger swaggers, staggers,
And haggard gold diggers pierce his sides with jeweled daggers -
Shades of Caligula, on the steps of the palace, are drawn by
nearsighted caricaturists
Working sidewalk cafés, outside rundown Catskill comedy clubs
on sultry summer nights -
All the while, the voluptuous torsos of unlucky magicians'
assistants are tucked sloppily away in plaid, polyester duffel bags.

The art of the one-liner has been lost -
Sound-bites at the heels of killer bees, migrating on cruise ships
Staffed by unhappy, virginal teenagers
Dreaming of sun-drenched sodomy, on olive-rich islands.

José, can you see if my entrée is ready?
Into the next world
Of demented, elderly passengers, sipping scopolamine-laced
mixed drinks, lecherous customs officials, and other assorted
spirits?

Here I sit,
In an unhygienic, yet still decidedly Edenic, garden,
Enjoying a colonic, while sipping lukewarm gin and tonic
On board the newly refurbished Biosphere III,
While scandalously malnourished, and knee-jerk, litigious
lobbyists
Scramble over ruined walls of ancient castles
On horses leased from great African kings,
In town for the weekend to catch a show -

Queen-sized in a world of disposable pawns,
Heaped in compost piles by pariahs living on state subsidies in
silver tunnels
Arranged like honeycombs by wild-eyed real estate developers.

Should we inhale the ants, as well, then?
Perhaps snort spiders, eh?
Rub ourselves in the skunk-scented bush?
Rush madly, unsolicited, and headlong into the thick trunks of
the already deeply contemptuous trees?
Don't misunderstand - I'm all for id. Ich lebe für das Es!
Florid, in point of fact -
A virtual Floridian,
A branch-spouting, fast-talking, pepper-spraying punk,
A barnacle on the ass of Christ,
Sun-dried, hemorrhoidal Puss in the skanky-ass panties of
eternity.

He who dies with the toast moist prospers most.

Fare ye well, my blue eyed son.
Your ill-starred train's about to stall.
Though cursed by your mother, and frozen in time,
Would it cost you that much to return her call?

If you were with me

Everything was a dry sawdust - Martian soil. Now it is wet, delicious - I can simply close my eyes, and the most delightful, sensuous, fluid images come dancing before me. The world tingles and vibrates. This is the me that you loved, and still love, if that other one has not destroyed that love. I pray he hasn't... If only I could hold onto this. If I could, I would be a happy, compassionate, and wise Bodhisattva. Jolly-old God has puckered his lips, blown dust from his cupped hands, and, miracle of miracles - the world has appeared - radiant, inviting, and warm. I am too content, and will pay for it (although hopefully have already paid for it, at least in part, recently). The world is now a delicious, warm, purple velvet - the snowflakes are twinkling feathers on radiant diamonds - everything is here, and the way it is, for a reason - if only to shimmer, to be painfully, rip-your-heart-out beautiful for a precious moment, a moment which sadly disappears the instant you attend to it.

You looked so beautiful last night - your smile and face infinitely young and pure - your soul both young and old - deep, and wise. The computer in front of me is different than it has ever been. I am right here - I hear it. It's unmistakable. But I have never heard it before. There's a gently beckoning world here, all the time - when the ceaseless chatter of my insides quiet down. It's right here - you and I are in it, all the time. Time goes forward, backwards, and stands still here - like an old, flat stick of gum, which has been rotting away in the pocket of one's pants unnoticed, but then suddenly balls itself up, and dissolves, in a riot of taste, in one's mouth - a taste latent within it all the time, through all of time, except that one had been unaware one had been carrying it, or even that one had taste buds at all.

Whatever chemical there is ordinarily too little of, there is now a flood of - I am happily drowning. The neurons which distinguish edges have been lazily and lovingly bathed in honey. I don't know where I stop and the air and world begin, nor do I want to know. If I could stay in this milky, swaying, ticklish world of dream forever, I would. If only you could be here too. Would that we might embrace - enveloped in white tendrils of clouds, plunged in the unearthly blues and greens of a tropic paradise, so that there was no longer any you and I, just the purest spark of consciousness - an infinite flame - above, behind, and beyond the here and now, and what we ordinarily call love. Can you join me here? Can you come? Will you come? Please, come. Please. It feels as if you're here with me, but there's this lonely hole in my guts, this hot tightness in my chest, that betrays you - that says you're not. If you were with me, you would understand. My soul would wrap itself around you, and we would dream together, enfolded in the serene embrace of God - only to awaken, slough off our cocoon, and emerge - winged and infinite.

It that a white rabbit in your hat, or are you just glad to see me? ♫

One girl makes it teeny,
And one girl makes it hard -
But the ones at the reunion
Look like wrinkled tubs of lard -
Go ask Phallus,
But not when he is...
Hard.

And if you go chasing pussy
When you're past a certain stage,
Chances are that you're the victim
Of either impotence or rage -
Go ask Phallus -
I think he'll say,
"Act your age."

When gals on the T.V.
Give you boners in your sleep,
But the women that are your age
Look like denizens of the deep -
Go ask Phallus -
I think he'll know.

When Time has trashed your body,
And you're bitter and forlorn -
When you're filled with misanthropy,
And you're even bored with porn -
Remember what that old whore said,
"You're half dead -
Go to bed."

It would have been a better world...

I know now, to my horror, that I could have left the Earth
A kinder, gentler landscape, with far fewer things to mourn -
If only I'd been strong, and not colluded in your birth!
We'd all be better off, for you would never have been born.

Or if you had been lifeless on that sad and fateful morn -
If from your mother's womb a stillborn infant had been torn,
Unable to embed itself in others like a thorn -
We'd all be better off, for you would never have been born.

You're not to ever set foot here! Your welcome's long outworn -
I won't keep all your filthy secrets, those to which I'd sworn -
And those who might approach you I'll be much compelled to
warn,
"It would have been a better world if you had not been born!"

For you I have no words of love or kindness, only scorn,
And when you're dead and gone, I will your victims all suborn
To show up at your grave, your granite marker to adorn
With words of hatred and the wish that you were never born.

Kaley

I met her online, in an AOL chat room, some 27 years ago. There was a great deal of misplaced initial excitement - she claimed to love philosophy, jazz, and still professed to be fascinated by the study of consciousness, even after 15 years as a neuroscientist. I knew full well that the "study of consciousness" was a sham, a young person's parlor game, a way to intellectually masturbate and pontificate in whatever manner one cared to, as the field consists of nothing other than quaint assertions sans evidence. And yet, that she claimed to be fascinated by anything was a draw for me - it implied she was a curious, passionate person. But it was all a lie - all of it. Her love of philosophy consisted of her having read a late Wittgenstein book in college, which she would later use in lazy, sham arguments to dismiss the rest of philosophy as meaningless language games, which had absolutely no interest for her, especially if I were presently reading said philosophy, and wanted to potentially discuss it with her. She had and has a profound lack of curiosity about absolutely everything. She was a good scientist, apparently, at least according to her, who came home, watched awful sit-coms, Hallmark movies, Shark Tank, American Idol, etc. (during which times it never once occurred to her to share the remote with her husband), read the same sorts of trash romance novels of which her mother was fond (whose cottage in Wisconsin was chock full of them), and whose intellectual level was therein reflected. Her father was purportedly a good jazz musician - once again, according to her. I'm far from unequipped to pass judgment in such matters. Although I never heard him play or improvise, I did see several of his "compositions". He was barely an amateur. This Dad died when she was 20, was duly canonized, and entered the official Schmidt Hall of Saints. Not long after, Kaley moved out East to study, because that's where all the pharmaceutical companies were and are - blithely leaving her cancer-ridden Mom in the care of her sister back in Wisconsin, a sister about whom she never had a kind word to say, and by whom she felt constantly angered and betrayed. The household mythology and ethos, as reported by the ever-unreliable <I-am-always-right-everyone else-is-a-villain> Kaley was that she had been the "good girl" during their childhoods. Why? Because that "bad" older sister, Ally, was constantly acting out. She dared to leave home at sixteen, to live with a "bad boy" in a bus, and even had a child with him. One would assume, or at least I would assume, that Ally left for reasons she found powerful and compelling, as in - her family was seriously disturbed, she never felt understood, and was neither valued nor respected by them. The reasons every kid runs away. And yet, years later, it was the "good sister" that deserted the mother, escaped to the East Coast when the going got bad, and then dumped the responsibility of taking care of their sick mother into the lap of that "bad" sister, the one who took their mom into her home, and cared for her during her last years and illness.

When I first visited Kaley at her home near the Passaic River, which routinely overflowed, ruining the carpets and much else besides, the entire place stunk of said filthy carpets and unchanged kitty litter. It was stuffed to the gills with the remnants and memories of her posthumously sainted parents. The apartment was a museum, a mausoleum - a shrine to an unconscious fantasy about perfect, blameless parents, parents from whom she ran away to go to graduate school, and to whom she never returned. This Miss Havisham-like existence continued, unabated, with no offers of compromise, when I chose to ignore all my healthier instincts, and moved in with her. Our entire house has always been that very same putrid landfill of garbage - the playground of a pathological hoarder, a hoarder who stuffs every shelf, and adorns every wall, with memories of those imaginary parents, a hoarder who still keeps her mother's ashes in a closet, twenty-seven years later, and who has deliberately left only infinitesimal amounts of space for me to put anything of my own - in order that I might have a chance to pretend that this is, in any sense whatsoever, my home too, who in fact never viewed me as anything other than a pawn in some unconscious mind game in which I was to represent the father whom she lost at twenty, the fourth-rate jazz musician, who had readily disowned the "bad" sister when she had had the chutzpah to assert herself as a person, as something other than a doll. When I met Kaley, I was still an active jazz musician. Several years into the relationship, I found myself playing, studying, and composing classical music more and more. It's what I'd gone to school for, after all. And, let's face it - it's superior music, in a multitude of ways. Her response? Her unironic response? "You got me using false advertising!" This was said perfectly seriously, without a hint of self-awareness. It was never about me, only what I could manage to do for her as a second-rate stand-in. I had dared to cease to be a viable mannequin, at least in that regard, a mannequin upon whom she could project the memory of her long-gone, not-really-jazz-musician father - a mortal sin, when one lives (exists) in the Schmidt Hall of Saints/mausoleum, with its self-appointed CEO and curator.

Kaley was forty when I met her, and had never had an actual boyfriend. She was no virgin, but mysteriously, all her love affairs were always with unavailable men who lived hundreds of miles away, or, in the case of her "first love", with whom she never lived either, a louse. Another villain. The world is divided, for her, along very predictable lines. There is Kaley (along with, eventually, her daughter, Evelyn), who is perfect, who has never, EVER uttered an apology, and then there is the rest of the world, which is populated by, at best, lower beings who disappoint her, but, more usually, by outright villains, whose ranks I eventually joined. I wore that badge of villainy more and more proudly, the more I wised up to the reality of this psychotic, toxic witch's Weltanschauung.

I was a mark, right from the start. Intended to play two roles - that of docile mannequin, who would roll over and willingly play his very small part in a ghastly, poorly written and conceived play, directed by ghosts, AND a sperminator, who could provide her with a child. She worked herself into an absolute frenzy chasing me down like prey, driving over two bridges when I wouldn't answer the phone, or slammed the door in her face after her having done so, ran down the stairs of subways, in order to escape her, many, many times, right in the heart of NYC, and on and on. Every intense, though barely understood, instinct I had to GET THE FUCK AWAY FROM HER was correct, was healthy, was a desperate clutching at what I knew was my threatened autonomy. I sensed what she was all about - the toxicity, the underlying agendas, the emptiness of her

Hallmark protestations - "Ours is the love of the millennium", etc. Are you freaking kidding me? Who the FUCK talks like that? I told her quite plainly that I was a trauma victim, and wouldn't be an easy boyfriend, but she persisted. In fact she redoubled her efforts, once she had heard that, for it was she who was going to "save me" through her monumental, cosmic love.

I had had four long-term, ACTUAL relationships, the kind where you actually share your souls, your interests, your bed (she has never slept in the same bed with me in 27 years, or the bed of any of her prior "boyfriends") - relationships in which you laugh and cry together, share EVERYTHING, create a LIFE together. None of them were perfect, by any means, but all of them were deep, true, nourishing, and long-lived. And, by the way, FUN. Kaley hasn't a clue what fun is, and possesses absolutely no sense of humor. I recall, with horror, the "lovemaking" in which we engaged those first few years. I knew, from a modest but reasonable amount of experience, that it can and should be fun, at least sometimes, like playing in a sandbox. With Kaley, it was eternally grim - full of her disingenuous, poorly acted displays of melancholy-faced vulnerability and deadly seriousness, about as believable as her "Ours is the love of the millennium" horseshit. Comical in retrospect, disgusting at the time.

I have only myself to blame. I ran, but she ran faster and harder, with nets of thick nylon rope in which she could bind, blind, and tame me. When someone incessantly love bombs a person with early childhood trauma, they are going to eventually succeed in wearing that person down. And this she did - blathering on with her insipid rescue fantasies, the promise to undo what had been done to me as a baby and toddler with her "cosmic love", blathering on with her treacherous lies about how she never wanted a child, but how, suddenly and miraculously, upon having met me, that it was her deepest wish, and that I was the one, the only one, with whom this was meant to be. For all eternity! I never wanted a freaking child, and was dead set on never having one. I grew up deeply traumatized in a hellish nightmare of a home, and was passionately committed to remain childless. But on and on it went, these bullshit tunes with their cheesy Hallmark lyrics, the unremitting love bombing, the constant promises and reassurances that I secretly, in my heart of hearts, did want a child. That I just didn't realize it - but how obvious it was to her, who could see all! It was relentless. The moonfaced, faux-soulful protestations, the laughably phony Spanish T.V. soap opera sex, the wistful, sad sack yearnings, cosmic and deep, obviously yet incompetently lifted from the trash romance novels so beloved by both mother and daughter.

This all lasted not very long - only up until the point when it was obvious she wanted to get pregnant, that is to say, ONLY wanted to get pregnant. No more twaddle re the "love of the millennium". She was on a mission to become a single mother, and she had found her mark. Minor setbacks were meaningless. Revealing her fangs? - that she would save for later. She took everything from me - my home, my flourishing piano teaching career, my independence, my health, my self. And I? I rolled over, I acquiesced, I let her take them. At whom am I most angry, most disgusted? With myself, naturally. And rightly so. If one were to meet a Komodo dragon in the park, even one wearing a fairly believable costume, one ought run the fuck away, no? I did my best to do so, and failed. The latter half of my life was, as a result, gleefully stolen from me.

Eventually, it became clear that we were not going to have a child naturally, so she organized the IVF. She paid for it (she made more money than I, and I was still fighting back - my ambivalence, terror, and attempts to flee were intermittently quite apparent). But by then I was a deer in the headlights, and had lost my sense of self. I was horrified when the IVF succeeded, and the greedy, venal fertility doctors shoved several embryos up her twat. I was still living two bridges away - I remember, quite vividly, the day I was to drive to New Jersey to go to the fertility clinic. I hung up on her several times, and finally said, "OK, I'll come to the fucking clinic and jerk off in a cup. Are you happy now?" Happy? Why, she was absolutely overjoyed! My feelings were utterly irrelevant - there was only the matter of what needed to be done. I was filled with what I'd like to call ambivalence, but that would not be correct - I was filled with self-loathing and horror, in full or at least unconscious knowledge that this was the last thing on Earth I wanted, that I had been manipulated and gaslighted into acquiescing to making her a single mother - her dream, from the outset. And when it succeeded? I knew I'd have to give up my career. I LOVED being a teacher and sometimes performer. It made me happy and fulfilled me. I gave up my 40 to 50 piano students, often over a dozen well-paying gigs a month, my freedom, my life, and my very self, to go live in New Jersey in a shrine to the dead - a landfill doubling as a tomb and mausoleum. I caved - this nightmare is all on me. It is my fault, due to my cowardice, and my falling for the love bombing and melodramatic, paper-thin, manipulative lie after lie after LIE. What did Kaley want? A docile sperminator, enabling her to become a single mother. And this is what I became, once the man I was had been annihilated - an embalmed trophy, sitting on an unattended shelf, in an overstuffed shrine to the unworthy, nay, evil dead. Eventually said mausoleum obtained a new acquisition - a completely unplayable 110-year-old 9 foot Steinway, which her saintly parents had acquired for nothing at a school giveaway - completely useless. A sarcophagus - nothing more. A monument to the long-deceased - more precisely to this madwoman's fantasy of the long-deceased. I met the mother at the end of her life. She was a nasty lady. "Does he know how impossible you are???" she said to her daughter, well within my earshot. Would that I had listened. Anti-semitic, Wisconsin white trash, all of them - no real interests, no curiosity, no depth, no sense of high art, literature, etc.

I had been pulled into a black widow's lair by a very, VERY savvy lady, who had intuited my psychological weaknesses, and was playing on them like a Stradivarius. So when she finally got pregnant, I moved to New Jersey, and promptly developed a MALT lymphoma in my stomach, which seemed to have concerned Kaley about as much as every other health issue with which I have ever had to contend - not at all. I had never tried to actually, utterly seriously off myself until I moved to New Jersey. I had had sometimes serious mental health issues intermittently before. The most notable bout with them occurred at the end of my first year of graduate school. And yet, in my thirties, while living with a gal with whom I wish I had stayed, I had not a one. It was the happiest, most carefree, and productive decade of my life.

When the IVF succeeded, the sex, unsurprisingly, stopped dead in its tracks. I endured "marriage therapy" for well over two years with a New-Age simpleton, who colluded with Kaley in every iteration of her "I am always right, and constantly disappointed and betrayed by everyone in my life, everyone around me who does not conform to my expectations and sense of entitlement." Especially guess who? Two years into this farce, I finally said no more, but agreed to see someone else. I did indeed find another therapist, but he made the fatal mistake of taking us both equally seriously, i.e., of being equitable. Kaley predictably bailed after two sessions. The nasty, hypercritical monologues, the endless harangues about her never getting what she needed from me, a monologue she repeated quite exactly, at lesser volumes, about practically everyone else in her life - her sister, her colleagues, etc. - these continued, unabated, to the present day. This is a woman with ZERO friends. She had two girlfriends whom she never saw, and whom she constantly complained of, for they were (surprise!) constantly disappointing her as well. From whence this bitterness? This inability to engage emotionally, spiritually, etc? This inability to love? Genes? Epigenetics? This parent, that parent, their combination? God only knows. Perhaps He cares. I fucking don't.

Evelyn was born before the marriage. I had to be dragged, kicking and screaming, to say "I do" under that tree of death. I regret the day I ever met Kaley, much less acquiesced to marry her. I mourn what I have lost, and what I have allowed to take place, which very much includes the birth of my daughter. Because that daughter, who was often a pleasure when she was small and remained "cute", gradually became her mother, whether it was a result of genes, endless maternal manipulations, or role modeling - who freaking knows. Or cares. She is an entitled, emotionally dysregulated, nasty, selfish, lacking all empathy, humorless piece of poo. And when that became increasingly apparent, ca. 14-15 yo, Kaley began a brutal campaign of triangulation and over-enmeshment, going to great, even criminal lengths to exclude me from her single parenthood, which had been, I am convinced, her goal from the very beginning. As this sick, poisonous, symbiotic relationship blossomed, like stinging nettle, into a pair of ambulatory Venus flytraps, I became progressively estranged from the two of them, out of disgust, and in an attempt at self-preservation. I could no longer bear her elaborately absurd Christmas and Thanksgiving rituals, which mirrored, quite exactly, those of her childhood - leaving reindeer food out for Rudolph on Christmas morning when Evelyn was twenty-one years old, etc.

Why did I not leave, even then? When I could, and was still healthy enough? When the vileness of the situation could not have become any clearer? Because I am a coward. I lack resilience and a sense of agency, both of which were stolen from me at a very young age. I don't offer these as excuses, only as observations.

In this house, where the perverse sounds and fumes of demons stomping on souls are so overwhelming, one hears the constant sounds of my 22 year old daughter, who now lives in Colorado with some poor schmuck, on the phone with her mother sometimes two or three hours a day, and the ping of her texting her mother sometimes thirty or forty times a day. And that's only how many times a day I hear the calls and texts COME IN, i.e., not the outgoing ones. In essence, or at least in part, parenting her mother, and courting absolute disaster when her mother leaves this earth - a mother who is doing to her own daughter precisely what her mother did to her. That poor schlemiel of a boyfriend. Perhaps he'll wise up - one hopes so, at least before they, GOD FORBID, make a baby upon whom to foist this sick, intergenerational nightmare. Who could, or would want to, write this play? Tennessee Williams? Perhaps. The "Glass Menagerie" contains hints of it. Edward Albee? Eugene O'Neill? But no. Why? Because the players are too inconsequential, too un-self-aware, too emotionally vapid and clueless, too hopelessly trivial. It doesn't, and could not possibly ever, rise to the level of real tragedy, because the cast never EVER have moments of insight into their own behaviors. In Sophocles, the characters may start out ignorant - of themselves, of what is to come, of their role in it - but the tragedy occurs when that revelation into themselves, and what they have done, crashes down upon them, inadvertently or not. This cannot happen in their upside-down fantasy world. They are both missing the human parts that would allow it to happen, for their eyes to look inwards and SEE. Would that I had only acted when my eyes opened, stayed open, and I could no longer look away.

Addendum -

"You are now expendable garbage, as a result of your unwillingness to play ball. You could have salvaged a small place at the end of the table, which my daughter and I share, as a sort of quaint appendage, had you fulfilled your duty as a cardboard stand-in for the father I lost at twenty years old, as the obedient, quiet jazz musician, who plays his pre-scripted part. But you wouldn't, or couldn't. You went about your business, studying things YOU wished to study, create things YOU wished to create - you went on being a separate person, one who was not entirely subject to my whims. And this was, and remains, unacceptable. And so, needless to say, I claim this child, this doll, this puppet, this plaything, as my own - to smother, suffocate, and condemn to the life I have lived - hopelessly alone, feeling constantly betrayed by everyone and everything other than my dead parents, who continue to smother and suffocate me posthumously, exactly as I will do to this already far-from-innocent child - now, and, when the time comes, like them, from beyond the grave. I shall remain, and she will become, lethally wounded, bitter, and friendless - an appendage, without a shred of curiosity, empathy, or humor, and utterly unable to love - the life my mother had, the one which she insured that I would have, and the one that I will make CERTAIN that she has, as well."

Late night thoughts while eating cheese blintzes with Aunt Rachel
(prior to a local screening of cries and whispers)

i saw the worst minds of my generation
belch breath mints,
gentle,
into the hothouse night.

oh, but how one's stomach grumbles,
one's heart burns, head aches,
the whole metaphysical magilla-
a life spent on the head of rusted pins,
bought sunday, in bulk, at walmart's
from nasty-ass cashiers -
under cheap, soul-crushing light fixtures,
fierce bemoaning their menstrual and writer's cramps,
their endless seven-year and jock-itch,
the seeming endless detritus and tsuris
of life's ass-fucked and horse-feathered labyrinth.
(just ask sadie if you don't believe me).

if a clock ticks in the forest,
and you fail to hear it,
will your zen master think you an idiot?
even though he is so often laser-focused
on his fast becoming unbearable need
to take an explosive piss?
admit it -
you never liked him anyway.

in the park, a troupe of merry elders
play a rousing game of arthritic leapfrog,
only to fall, laughing, in a heap of jangled cartilage -
hi-ho! the dingle bloody!
see them don their pungent sleep-masks
and hold hands
to sing the dreadful folk-songs of their youth -

their cold farts resonating
beneath a soggy and sluttish moon.

the masters advise one to keep
meticulous and copious dream-journals and diaries -
only in this way is one assured of living on after one's death,
if only for that one brief guilt-ridden moment
your children will experience
when discarding them.

fish have it made, existentially speaking -
to live in one's shit, yet never to notice,
much less care.

dogs express their affection with dignity and reserve,
sensitive as they are to the "ick" factor,
which inevitably arises from prolonged contact,
even between members of different species -
as opposed to, say,
your massively bosomy aunt sophie,
who recognizes no such boundaries.

yes, yes, that sparrow there -
a modern-day dinosaur, he -
what science has yet to quantify is:
exactly how pissed the little fucker is about it.

in the country of old men,
the TV's are both
tuned to no particular channel,
and ungodly loud.

i have been to a mountain or two,
yet had no dream worth repeating,
although
i do recall that one nasty bout of altitude sickness.

we humans are, after all,
finally,
only thelma and louise,
writ small, and bare-knuckled,
in the metaphysical henhouse of doom-
except,
as sartre might have observed,
we are neither brave,
nor are our looks anything to write home about.

and, finally,
thank you, jesus -
without your grisly wounds and ghastly suffering,
this computer would almost certainly never have been made
by slave workers in china -
(oh, and - thanks, mum and dad -
for your constant needling,
violent, psychotic outbursts,
and pathological narcissism.)

and then of course there is you, dearest reader -
thank you for the once passionate idealism of your strapping
youth,
now withered to a paltry stalk of received wisdom -
croaked frog-like, over stale pastries,
between the rude and deeply unappetizing belches
of your meshuga relatives.

Mein armer, gebrochener Vater

I was in the garage that morning, chatting with Dad about the raccoon trap I had found in the eaves of the attic the previous day. I asked him if it was true that my mother used to put my pacifier in there. Was this a memory, a fantasy? There was no question that it was a recurring nightmare. Was there anything to it?

"I think it's just perverse family mythology, Son. I wouldn't give it much credence."

"But Dad - I'm looking at the proportions of the trap. Why do the scar and gash in my leg that I've had ever since I can remember seem to exactly correspond to this thing's teeth?"

"I suppose it could've happened, Son. Honestly, I had headphones on the first twenty years of the marriage. Every so often, your mother would bang on the door of that back room, you know the one - the one in which I hid myself constantly. She would burst in, rip them off, start shrieking that I had destroyed her life, and threaten suicide. It could very well have happened without my being aware of it."

"But that said, I do need your opinion on something. I know you don't particularly care for me talking about these sorts of things, but where else can I turn? You're a big boy. You're MY big boy, and I love you. Anyway, when I try to adjust the vacuum pump I'm using to get something vaguely resembling an erection with Selma - you met Selma, right? What did you think of her? Sometimes I see her rifling through my credit cards while she's pretending to fix her make up, which has inevitably run all over her craggy, battle-ax face. Do you think there's anything suspicious in that? I've ignored it up till now. But forget about that - that's not what I want to pick your brain about. When all those horrendous, whooshing and sucking noises finally begin to die down, and I'm standing there at half-mast, ready to at least give it the old college try, she always interrupts and croaks, in that godforsaken cackle of hers, something more or less like - 'Maybe later, honey, we'll see. Let's discuss where you're going to take me to eat tonight. I hope it's not that cheap Guinea joint again. I mean really - we can do better than that, can't we?'"

"I don't really see any harm in it, Dad. I'm quite sure her intentions are noble. It's clear she likes you for you."

"And then, predictably, like clockwork, your mother will call - screaming that her check is five minutes late, or that her lower intestine has just slid out of her body and into the toilet because of her Crohn's, or is wrapped around her throat, how she's ready to jump out her second-story window, how that's obviously my fault, and how she wishes that me and all my rat bastard girlfriends would rot in hell. Look, you know me - I always take the high road. I'm not trying to demonize her, or get you to take sides, but the truth is that, for most of the marriage, she had electrodes attached to my testicles, and carried the remote around with her, no matter where we went - out to eat, the pool - anywhere and everywhere. And you must remember how she used to put fruit pits in those gummy bread balls she would stick in her inedible meatloaf, hoping you or I would break our teeth on them. She told me all the time, and you, several times, that she wished you had never been born - lamenting that you hadn't been born a card-carrying lesbian like your sister. She actually tried to snip your pee-pee off those first few weeks, but was too weak and depressed. Later, when she was feeling more herself - well, you remember all the sexual abuse, the constant intimidation and humiliation - I needn't remind you. What you may not remember, because you were so young, is that she would frequently drop the three pairs of leggings that you were forced to wear, even in the summer, in the middle of town, and squawk, so all around could hear, 'What the hell is the matter with you? You have to make a wee-wee, NOW???' Of course, you had not given her the slightest indication that you had to make a 'wee-wee'. But look - this is a woman that overfed her poor Dachshund, Jezebel, until she could barely move - until her fat guts bled until they were like raw meat from scraping the sidewalk. She stuffed you with food, as well, till you couldn't move - any attempt to do so on your part was met with three additional layers of leggings, and a good smack in the face. And, of course, as was true then, and is true now - she weighed about ninety-pounds, looked like an Auschwitz inmate, and lay in bed complaining of her back pain from dawn to dusk. As for me, I didn't know where to turn for self-esteem. I would lose myself at the office as best I could - unless and until my Dad, the president, would call or arrive in that office to yell at me that I was an incompetent loser and disgrace. This is the Dad that yanked me off the track to be an English professor, which would almost certainly have made me happy and fulfilled, sufficiently happy and fulfilled that I doubt I would have ever even considered ending up with your mother. Yes, yes - I did beat the crap out of you, at her behest, a bunch of times - I admit it. And you remember it perfectly well, whether I admit it or not. I feel awful about that now, Son. I am so, so sorry. I tried to have a social life - to get off that bed of death on which she lay. I used to drive my Harley over to Ghost Motorcycles, to burp and fart with all the other middle-aged, fat, balding losers - it was better than nothing, I suppose. But then I'd return - and your mother would be laying there like death, not even remotely warmed-over, just death - Death - a shriveled, shrunken, withered 35-year-old corpse with the skin of an ancient shoe. I could've been someone. I was summa cum laude, phi beta kappa, I could've been someone. I was on the way to being someone. But she and my father ruined my life, squelched all my potential, and made me give up all my aspirations. Sometimes I think it's my fault - I did roll over, acquiesce. Other times, I'm more forgiving. It felt hopeless and inevitable, like a thousand albatross were gnawing constantly on my neck. What could I do? I don't think I read a single thing besides the crappy newspapers I delivered for a living for 20 years while I lay on that bed, night after night (me - a lover of Shakespeare, Dostoyevsky, and Yeats), with the TV blaring lowbrow trash - next to that misshapen miscreant, that inhuman, endlessly vindictive creature, with her interminable complaints of back pain, which were all bullshit. We both know that. We both saw her staggering in pain when she thought she had an audience, and scampering down the hall like Baryshnikov when she felt confident no one was watching. If only, if only. Well - at least now I have a few years left, and am free."

"But Dad - the truth is you've only and ever been attracted to cruel, despicable women, at that time, and ever since. I'm sure it has nothing to do with your own mom, who was a psychotic sadist - who took great pleasure verbally castrating her husband, and lacerating his guts - that is, when she wasn't busy chloroforming some pathetic, innocent Great Dane puppy, whom she deemed wasn't up to breed standards, or shrieking at some poor black lady, who who had the misfortune of working for her.

But here's the real rub - with all the obvious psychosis in your family, and with a certifiable, hateful lunatic for a mother, how did you emerge as a simply messed up-guy who made bad, cowardly choices, but who has a heart, a soul, who loves music and literature and great thinkers? (when you're not drowning your brain in rotgut booze, at any rate) And why did my mother, whose mother was, yes, judgmental and sometimes cruel, but more or less a resident on Planet Earth, whose father was the quintessential, literally eat-his-own-guts-apart martyr, saint, and perfect sweetheart (WARNING, WARNING - no such animal exists - this sort of thing is always a disguise for God knows what sinister secrets), and a sister who is sweet, kind, and, at worst, a bit of an airhead - why did my mother become that brutal, monstrous, heartless demon she is now and was during all my growing up? You I understand. You I love. You I forgive. Her I do not understand, shall never understand, and do not wish to understand. My only wish now is to create myself anew, finally - now that I am free of being enveloped in her sick, poison-infested tendrils. And yet, and yet - I see and feel all the loss and rage and impossible pain in all I've just said. I may never escape it. How can I fix it?"

"Here, Son, try this Jack Daniels. Selma will be here soon."

Miriam

Miriam was born with an ice-cold spatula in her womb. Her mom had repeatedly warned her that the neighbors' dog would eat her liver unless she walked backwards from school every day while repeating her intention to gain six pounds by week's end, and, upon her return, ritualistically sprinkled mothballs around the perimeter of the house. Friendless and alone, she dutifully practiced her Hanon and Schumann every night in preparation for her Saturday morning piano lesson, at which time Mr. Hugo would inevitably insult her mercilessly and then expose himself.

Confronted with the specter of poverty and spinsterhood, she grimaced, found a broken man with a rich dad, who consented to marry her, and bore two severely deformed children, who meant less than nothing to her. The Karen Ann Quinlan of the Brown University Class of '52, she floated, for the next 20 years, in more or less dreamless sleep, in which her vitriol and despondency expressed itself only through her frequent grunts, scowls, and violent myoclonic jerks. Her husband read the paper as the bedsores festered, and the IV dripped. One day, for no particular reason, she awoke to a world in which every ladybug and falling leaf was fraught with urgent meaning for her and her alone. Lonely no longer, she stared intently into the filament of lightbulbs, and read all the tea leaves which had miraculously appeared in the swirling woodgrain of her night table. She bought a microscope and spent hours counting the dust mites on her eternally unwashed pillow. The sun, moon, stars, and even her much-loathed neighbor, Mrs. Epstein, now existed only to perpetually watch her, revere her, and hover above her like guardian angels - in life, in sleep, and in death.

One day, as she climbed down the stairs tentatively, her long, uncut nails boring into the railing, in order to prepare her breakfast of five pieces of still-frozen cut broccoli and one-third of a slice of white toast, her cells froze and she crashed onto the linoleum kitchen floor, where her husband later found a thousand hooked and twisted shards of glass.

Miscellaneous observations

HYPOTHESIS: Every day/hour/moment is subjectively experienced as lasting whatever fraction it constitutes of one's life up until that point.

RESULT OF THOUGHT EXPERIMENT: The subjective midpoint of an average seventy-five year life-span is approximately 4.5 years.

CONCLUSION: SHIT!!!

If we are, as Richard Dawkins more or less proposes, meat puppets, which have evolved strictly for the purpose of ferrying selfish genes from one generation to the next, everything makes perfect sense - the proportions of pleasure and pain in the world, and the seasons of life in which we are more apt to experience the one or the other. There is no need to bother with notions of good and evil, inscrutable divine plans/wills, and all that other, dubious at best, unquantifiable, fairytale horseshit. Pure naked power. Nietzsche would have loved it. Especially if Nietzsche had been a transposase.

It's kinda dark, but reality is always helpful (as my first shrink remarked, memorably, almost forty years ago), and to embrace something with such vast explanatory power is, for me at least, somehow consoling.

Many, if not most Western philosophers believe in free will. Science has conclusively demonstrated that free will, at least our every day notion of it, is a fiction. Existentialism, in particular, depends upon man's ability to radically choose. Hence, teaching Existentialism in the schools is tantamount to teaching Creationism, or Alchemy. I propose we begin furiously writing and petitioning university administrations to institute an immediate ban on the teaching of Existentialism.

The National Enquirer reports that Hillary Clinton is facing severe health issues, sufficient to make her question her religious faith. I sincerely hope the former is not the case, but, for the sake of a simple thought experiment, let's suppose the latter is the case. That would imply that a woman, who, as Secretary of State, has privileged information about, and witnessed the aftermaths of, the most appalling atrocities and human tragedies, only began to doubt the existence of God in the face of her own suffering. Hopefully this is not the case with Mrs. Clinton, but we know it is, or has been, the case for countless "people of faith". The conclusion being...

Isn't it amazing how the greatest musical achievements in the history of Western Civilization (just ask any connoisseur or critic) just happened to have been penned within the last two or three hundred years? Aren't we fantastically, cosmically lucky? What an awesome and fortuitous coincidence! It's up there with Jesus Christ, our Lord and Savior, just having happened to be born a couple of millennia before your and my lifetimes. After 4 1/2 billion years.

Stravinsky said he was the vessel through which the Rite of Spring passed. But he could have said exactly the same thing about his following through on his urge to have a pastrami sandwich that afternoon. Although it doesn't sound as impressive, it's no less true, and just as miraculous, in its own way.

PROOF: Tonal music is more complex, expressive, and rich in meaning than atonal music.
AXIOMS REQUIRED:
The ability of a single part, in any given style, to convey meaningful information is predictive of that style's ability to do so.
A monophonic serial piece would, necessarily, be absurd, given that a truly serial piece would have no legitimate reason to continue after having exhausted its twelve notes.
A monophonic, atonal piece cannot imply more than one part without referencing the procedures of tonal music.
Monophonic tonal pieces routinely imply two, three, and even four parts.

THEREFORE: Tonal music is necessarily more complex, expressive, and rich in meaning than atonal music.
QED

PLEASE PRESENT THE FOLLOWING COMPLETED QUESTIONNAIRE TO ST. PETER UPON ARRIVAL -

Any kindnesses performed or good deeds done

Plus - The couple of dozen moments of inspiration, if you're lucky, which have occurred during your lifetime

Plus or minus - The number and moral characters of children you've brought into the world (take particular care to be honest re the net positives and negatives here)

Minus - The land rendered barren, and/or infertile by the production of your food (please use metric measurements)

Minus - The plant(?) and animal suffering and death involved in producing said food

Minus - Your contributions to global warming

Minus - Your contributions to other forms of pollution, e.g., non-recyclable waste, etc.

Minus - The suffering experienced by the less fortunate to make your first-world lifestyle possible

Minus - The number and types of bodily excretions, unpleasant body odors, etc., that you have produced over your lifetime

Minus - Any bad or unkind shit you've done

Add up all of the above, and you will arrive at "Your Legacy as a Human Being on Planet Earth".

N.B. Add three points to your total, if you did not specifically request to be born. You may also list any mitigating circumstances which you feel are relevant on the reverse side of this questionnaire.

Dried pee on doggy paws smells like buttered popcorn. I have pondered long and hard upon this mystery, ever since my little sister pointed it out to me over 40 years ago, and have finally concluded that it is, indeed, a miracle.

Am I a man or a mouse? Not a particularly interesting question. Far more interesting is whether God is a dog or a cat. Let's think this through... God calls to us through painful and debilitating illness, the fear and depression associated with same, and old age. He devours us, at those times, in moments, or extended moments, of paralyzing terror and death agonies. I'd say that makes him, pretty much for sure, a cat, a nasty ass cat. And the rest of us, um..., yeah – pretty much mice.

I remember lying, endlessly, night after summer night, in Kings Point Park, next to my eventual first girlfriend - never touching, growing ever closer. I remember her finally touching me, after six weeks of my what seemed hopeless sheepishness and fear, and the agonizing knowledge that she was someone else's. I remember the taste of the wind, the smell of the dirt and leaves, her every last word, her every touch, every inch of her skin, every bead of her perspiration... I remember the feeling of being one with everything - with her, with the night sky, with the universe... I remember getting the shit beaten out of me by my parents, because I had stayed out all night. I remember either not feeling it, or not caring in the slightest, for I had tasted of the infinite - of pure goodness, of what seemed and tasted like a divine love.

I remember how, in the first flush of Wagner-mania, I stayed up all through the night, listening to the entire Ring, dutifully following the orchestral scores. I remember how the first rays of dawn peaked through the window at the very moment the sun revealed Siegfried's and Brünnhilde's rock in the Götterdämmerung prologue. I remember my spine exploding, the feeling of the leather couch, its every crevice, every shivering joint and tendon of my body, the feeling that the apartment had no roof, that I was bodiless, and spinning through endless space.

I remember returning home from a gig at twenty-seven years old, walking from the train, and eventually jumping effortlessly over a high fence, all lean and wolfish. I remember the feeling of endless vibrancy, potency, mastery, the full flush of youth. The rapturous blood, nerve, and sinew. I remember that feeling too soon subverted by the poignant thought that it would never be this good again. My body, at any rate.

I remember a similar return home from the train, in which I stopped dead in my tracks before an enormous oak tree, which was, unquestionably and purposefully, communicating with me. Not thoughts, not ideas - just ten minutes of deep, delirious, oceanic consciousness, which it naturally and eternally possessed, and was, for whatever reason, kindly sharing with me for those moments, and those moments only.

I remember those manic, completely sleepless couple of weeks, the days and nights in which I sketched out 24 songs to words of Stevie Smith - the unerring feeling of exactly when to end the nighttime walk because the inspiration was about to whoosh back upon me, the smell of the diner to which I would walk at 4 a.m, because I often had not eaten in two days, the smell and taste of the eggs, every word, glance, and expression of the poignantly sad, tired, and resigned waitress, and the strange, bedraggled, somewhat scary-looking fellow at the counter - his greasy hair, scars, tattoos, cigarettes, and weirdly sad mutterings. Both of whom were exquisitely beautiful and perfect because the world, too, for those couple of weeks, was exquisitely beautiful and perfect - those minutes, days, nights, and weeks burned into my brain, forever. Why those moments, and not other, more specifically creative moments, I do not know. The eye of an ecstatic hurricane, perhaps.

I remember holding my still bloody, mucus-drenched daughter for the first time - those eternal instants of first bonding, and my long-suffering wife, with crystalline tears of joy rolling down her face. I remember feeling, knowing that something was eternal, that how, in the barter of birth, one becomes merely a vessel and nurturer, and, somehow, suddenly matters far less than before, and how that was exactly as it should be - cosmically right, and profoundly consoling. These feelings and knowings were not accompanied by subvocalized thoughts, no, not at all - but as some sort of depersonalized telepathy with something infinite - as a communion, as a welcome casting off of the ravaged self.

Last night, our beloved Lab, Charlie Parker Brown, climbed in bed. I woke with my hand on his belly, feeling his beating heart. Every so often he would flinch - wild dreams in the pitch blackness.

We are all fretting little pinheads, nothing more - busy taking ourselves so very seriously, poking out just a hair's breadth atop the blind, ravenous, pulsating universe, of and in which we are slaves.

I see the boys and girls of spring in the grassy meadow, with their awkward tuxedos, slit prom dresses, their trashy, pink limousines, their proud, and often justly horrified parents - staring at one another when they can, averting their eyes and gaze when they must. I see their future children, greedily hovering behind their lustful eyes, and hear those children's cries, their unrelenting clamor to be born, wafting uneasily through the breeze.

The dead squirrel in the park. Who, for a time, carried the entire world in his little brain. He was fast disappearing, little by little, and today was, finally, gone. Perhaps his friends will miss him for a time. Perhaps he had a name his friends used to call him - perhaps he had dreams, goals, wishes, family…
The dreaming earth. The dead are free.

Molly
Chapter I

We met one another at a diner, a block from Desiree's little studio apartment, as I was to learn later. I had taken the train in from Long Island to meet her - we had exchanged more or less pleasant emails enough times to be modestly optimistic about arranging a meeting. And New York City was such a source of comfort to me - I love walking about anonymously in a sea of people whom I can freely observe without fear. It seems a gigantic circus, constructed specifically for my amusement - my superficial and quite unjustifiable analyses, judgments, and conclusions concerning others. It feeds my gargantuan, voyeuristic hunger. Truth be told, however, I had this painful aching to fall in love - that was what was driving me, over and above everything else: the hunger to feel something I had not felt in years, or, perhaps, had never felt. There was a beast awakening in me - needy and ravenous.

I had been living and sleeping with Molly for going on nine years. We had bought a house in the suburbs together three years ago. I cherished our mindless domesticity - it was bliss, what with our two wonderful dogs, her innocent, cherubic face, her smile, her pleasant greeting at the end of the day, the seeming security of it all. I felt satisfied with the comfort and predictability, in a way I had never experienced in life. And yet, concealed deeply within this peace, in this stability, in this very house, lurked the potential for torrential upheavals - upheavals which would end in horrendous psychological violence, the likes of which I could never have imagined.

Molly mirrored and reinforced every wish of mine to withdraw from the world at large - to isolate and alienate myself from others out of fear and condescension, a condescension which was almost certainly borne of fear. Every hysterical outburst and tantrum of mine was tempered by her lack of ability to respond in kind. Or was this equanimity, in fact, her choice, her conscious choice - a pose of some kind? And herein lay her profound mystery and deep appeal. That's what it was for me, really, the mystery of a person who seemingly was able to live in an affectless world - in a perpetual, sublime, almost God-like state of narcissism, unruffled by any and all slings and arrows that might come her way. She did have her social fears - her shyness, her obsessions with appearance, and the opinions of others. Yet she possessed, as far as I was able to intuit, no sense of the tragedy of life - of the grim, painful cycle of birth, need, attachment, loss, betrayal, isolation, love, hate, and death. No grief, no joy. She was inexplicable, utterly. A mannequin with a sweet smile and, seemingly, no soul. Exactly what I most wished for after Katy died - although it must also be said that this mannequin had another side which expressed its haughty sadism in the tone of a critical, reprimanding, and condescending mother. Either this character trait had been growing at a phenomenal rate these past few months, or it had always been there - and I was just growing ever more aware of, resentful of, and disgusted by it.

On my first date with Molly, I knew intuitively that I was in the presence of a being who was better defended, and more completely and hopelessly repressed than anyone I had ever known. As I came to discover more about her family, I came to see her as a defeated, fractional creature, who was missing a host of very basic human attributes, who had been blessed with, or had created, by an act of pure will, enough armor to enable her to survive - in the face of the most horrid and devastating family circumstances one could imagine. In this I found, paradoxically, a great deal to admire and a great deal to be horrified by. There was, however, no question that the disembodied emptiness of her interior world was sedating and narcotic for me - a deep, opiated incense, an invitation to dive headfirst into a perfect, painless world - a world where one is "dead while alive" - a Zen phrase, which had caught my attention as an adolescent, had stayed with me since that time, and which I now find utterly repugnant - repugnant in the ways in which Nietzsche, of whom I am no fan, would have found it repugnant.

Well then - here was a modern day Zen master, a survivor of many a holocaust, which would have ripped most folks to psychological shreds - AND/OR - a terrified little girl, who had been lucky enough to stumble upon the eye of the hurricane, to understandably bolt and lock the doors, and then busy herself with setting up psychological shop within its safe borders. Balance inside, in a world out of balance. One could even judge others from the safety of such a vantage point - transmute one's paranoia into grandiosity and condescension, like some sort of medieval alchemist. And yet, I experienced (I, who should have known better, my grandiosity insists) in my peaceful days living with Molly, happiness and security of a sort I had never known, and of which I found it difficult to believe I was capable or worthy. Life with a porcelain angel - an insinuating, intoxicating pool of lies, in which I was more than happy to drown.

This gnawing panic, this mushrooming intuition that something was terribly wrong, catapulted me onto the computer, the romance boards, and, eventually, to this diner. Point, click... blind date! Point, click... endlessly inappropriate, outright foolish projections and idealizations! The computer was a terribly seductive little contraption. I had already succumbed, only a month ago, to a hysterical online romance, in which the most melodramatic exchanges, absurd protestations, and embarrassingly purple and pretentious creative writings had had me head over modem in love - with a screen name. Needless to say, the denouement of that "relationship" was painful and disappointing - and yet I was grateful to the woman for what our cyber-tryst had helped clarify - that which had been missing from my life: smoldering adolescent passion - the fantasy of oceanic connection with a woman, all wrapped up in a pretentious, juvenile, 19th century Wagnerian ethos. This is who I had been when a young man - I, who, since that time, went on to be plagued with black depression, unspeakable loss, widowhood, and the sense that I now roamed the Earth as a sort of voyeuristic ghost...

I would often reflect upon how astounding it was that our relationship had survived up until this point, given that it was so vacuous on so many levels. And yet she was the perfect woman for me, and for the longest time. I, too, had become, somehow, quasi-angelic - in ways obviously too good to be true - numb to my core after my wife Katy's death - pliable, seemingly good-natured, tame, unworldly, rattled by nothing. I felt that my life, after her death, had a curious "posthumous" quality to it - voyeuristic, spectral, as if I were indeed that wraith walking unseen amongst the living - observing, watching. Molly was the angel who lit up the dark despair following my wife's death. And she even somewhat resembled Katy and I physically, truth be told. She was the perfect vehicle for my projections. We possessed no intellectual or emotional similarity - none that I was aware of or could observe, at any rate. Perhaps, in being the frequently emotional, hysterical, and melodramatic engine of our relationship, I had robbed her of the chance to express other parts of herself. Perhaps I was a curse, perhaps a blessing - as was she, for me. Perhaps, and more likely, both.

My desire for passion began to ignite around that time. And yet, along with that, I could simultaneously look at almost any woman, any reasonable-looking woman, and imagine that she was but a single, small, visible point in a vast universe - connected in some mysterious way to a sort of Platonic Idea of "Woman." The longing for one seemed the longing for another, and, underlying both, lay the longing to be submerged in all - the longing for oblivion, a very old longing, one of the very first I experienced in life. Perhaps this was a profound, oceanic insight - perhaps a poorly articulated bit of nonsense, coughed up from a vat of defective brain chemistry. After all, I'd been a mental patient in my early 20s - a victim of deeply debilitating, suicidal depression, a veteran of the medication parlor games of godawful, clueless physicians, of the ECT table, et al. And although I functioned at a more or less predictably professional level of expertise in my piano teaching, the beast constantly hovered over my shoulder, periodically grabbing me by the throat. Hypnagogic, oceanic, dissociative experiences of persons, nature, feelings, and of cruel, indescribable suffering were familiar, though most unwelcome, companions.

My life has never been my own. My moods are dictatorial, overwhelming. Projects have to be completed with a ferocious immediacy, or they are apt to remain unfinished - quickly forgotten sketches. Mine is the queasy, paranoid obsessiveness of the insomniac, who knows he might well lose everything momentarily - the slim thread generating his fleeting creativity, and the often ephemeral cognitive strength to carry it through. Large-scale projects have always been out of the question. For me, there are only jottings - songs, poems, short pieces… I must impale my ideas to the workbench - become an obsessed, bleary-eyed maniac, who cannot and will not rest - for I know those ideas may, at any time, disperse like smoke into a barren, wind-whipped sky. Moods have always been my reality, far more than the outside world. The comings and goings of others have always been unreal for me - observed, as they were and still are, through a pane of glass - ever since I was a small boy and the neighbors whooped, splashed, and shrieked in their above-ground pool across the street, and I looked on, a shadowy phantom, peering through a basement window I was barely tall enough to negotiate. I was then, and have been ever since, all the while watching, from behind that pane of glass - already "posthumous", betrayed, at five years old, in some irrevocable way - cut off from the stream of life, not even desirous of it, not even able to imagine being desirous of it - already beginning to acclimate to my role as spectral outcast. What is outside my skin, and what is within it, what is here, what is "me" - these are things that were never to have intimate knowledge of one another.

Of course, that was Molly's appeal. Her attraction consisted in her being, in some profound sense, the same as I - and yet, at the same time, far superior to me, in that she had discovered how to be at peace with it all - how to be comfortable shutting down the the engine, the entire system. My adolescent flirtations with Zen, TM, Schopenhauer, Wagner… What were all those things, if not feeble, unsuccessful attempts to achieve what this angelic Scottish milkmaid, with her simple, mindless smile, and long ago emptied-out insides, had achieved far earlier, more easily, and more profoundly in her own life?

But lately, fits of sobbing at the slightest pretense of a provocation, or, worse, without any such provocation, would bring the white-hot lava of long-buried, visceral emotions streaming into my consciousness. They had always been there, of course, during the best of times, peeking out from just behind a half-closed door - ready, when the moment seemed appropriate, to rush upon me like an avalanche of psychic need, bile, pain, rage - and utter helplessness. An infinite, bleeding, ever-raw wound - unfixable and seemingly eternal.

To perceive of the universe as being purposeful, as being good, just - a cosmic school with, who knows, graduations and grades... What a sublime gift! Could there be a human being luckier than this naïve, artless woman, who believed such things, such utter nonsense? To believe the world is a moral and just place requires fabrications, blindness, and monumental projection upon projection. If only I had skills this sophisticated and effective! I spent close to ten years drinking them in, bathing myself in their narcotic waters. Ultimately the sad truth of who I'd been all along made its appearance - the portent and guarantee of the road to Hell on which I was now to travel.

What was I doing here, meeting Desiree at the Cinema Diner? What did I want? I was hungry, and not for their crappy food - that was obvious. I was terribly unsure of what it was that might be available on the battered, scarred menu of approaching midlife. I had to see, though. I had to see if I could be nourished by or possessed the wish to nourish another being. Hunger and meaning seemed inextricably entwined in me, although, periodically, a good, hard, cold look at the world tended to disabuse me of such optimistic fantasies. Love had always seemed, to me, to matter most, to be woven into the fabric of the universe - an all-encompassing, oblivion-laced love, into which one dissolved. Love and beauty... Honor, pride, justice, success, "truth", et al. - those things meant less than nothing to me - nor do they now. I don't live in the adult world - the world of civic responsibility, in which one votes, believes in the self-evident importance of thought, culture, "humanity", in which one prides oneself on one's civilized decorum. Justice, honor, morality... These things seem, to me, downright mythological. Hadn't Postmodernism signaled the end of everything? The end of history, of patriotism, of moral precepts? The end of meaning is not a subject to be bandied about only by overfed, privileged brats and tenured, burnt-out professors behind Ivy-coated walls, but, rather, it was intended and destined to encourage ecstatic chaos and violence in a godless, amoral world. Or so I wished to believe. Read Sade - it's all there. Every bit of "meaning", every "value", every piece of demagogic morality is nothing other than the foul carcass of an albatross, sewn on clueless shoulders, and unwittingly borne by the individual in society. But these thoughts are old hat. It's only that I LIVED them. I walked through Manhattan, and everything was clear to me. I found the human race absurd and laughable, those high falutin' lemurs with their briefcases and big ideas about themselves, ideas about their uniqueness and importance in the grand scheme of things, with their self-absorbed, grandiose, religious stories, scientific stories, etc. - and, underneath and driving it all, their terror of dying.

I lived, and continue to live, in a world where creatures are acted upon - where beings create retrospective fictions to explain their necessary, determined thoughts and actions - calling them "decisions" and "choices" - the laughable creations and fictions of false "selves". Whether the universe is necessary, or the product of quantum, random probability, or of pure chance - none of that remotely matters. Human notions of morality, cause and effect, and "justice" are all a joke - whether we are marionettes controlled by a perverse God, or rag dolls, violently thrown about by mindless, random winds.

This hunger, this woman, Desiree - this charming, lovely, very large-breasted woman sitting across from me - this obviously very bright, and disarmingly open woman. Well then - this was a game in which I wanted to be a player. These games used to seem a matter of life and death - of souls, soulmates, eternity... now they were games in my presently posthumous existence - an uncanny world of memory, numbness, and distant, near-forgotten hopes, now unseen and inaudible.

My wife Katy's ghost hovered over the proceedings - forcing subliminal comparisons, guilt, and, most of all, resentment at her presence. Perhaps I could somehow revive her through the gradually increasing abuse of prescribed substances, and the loss of my will to live. Unlikely, but a fantasy nonetheless. I was, to her, among other things, many other things, a fly in the web of her charisma, her volatility, her anger, a tree branch in the hurricane which swarmed around her, eyeless. She told me I made her want to live. My knowledge of her didn't support that statement. Nor did subsequent events. She lived, rather, to torment her parents with guilt - to force them to demonstrate towards her an impossible, unconditional, bottomless love. Katy lived, to a very large extent, for retribution - to settle an old score with her mother, who had exhibited disgust and withdrawn emotionally from her during her early life, when Katy's food allergies had caused her to soil herself constantly with foul-smelling excrement. Katy lived to censure and inflict pain upon this woman. Her father, on the other hand, loved her more than life. At the same time, he loved his wife, his life, himself, not very much at all. I believe Katy's mother actually despised her. I believe she despised the competition for attention which Katy's frequent borderline theatrics created. I remember very vividly, like it was yesterday, how the mother practically immolated herself upon her daughter's open casket - sobbing, like a Greek tragedienne - "My baby, my baby!", upon viewing her corpse in an open casket at the funeral home, the night before the funeral itself. She began this likely rehearsed and then re-rehearsed display of melodrama and exhibitionism so early upon entering the room where Katy's body lay that the echoes of her cries in that large room dropped like wet dung to the floor - unresonant, and hopelessly false. Whatever grief she bore was for herself, and herself only. I realize that I am painting here a portrait of an impossible harpy, and that there are none in our world, unredeemed by other qualities, or, at least, excused by their own damage. But there are those who take upon themselves the responsibility of parenting, whose estimations of themselves and their abilities verge on the delusional. And there are those who have the dignity to admit they are less than well-equipped to foster, nurture, and shape the character of some freshly spat out, unfortunate being, who would have much preferred to stay in the painless anonymity of the ether - or who will at least admit, in retrospect, and with great sadness, that they failed at it, and should never have flirted with the chance of creating such horrid suffering in the first place. They maintain a sort of dignity to which the blind can never aspire. And never do aspire.

Was this woman, who sat across from me at the Cinema Diner, a milder, more self-possessed, more articulate Katy? She reminded me a great deal of my first girlfriend, Alice, physically, although she was far lovelier. After nine years of living in gray oblivion with a mannequin and lying in bed with a corpse, she seemed the sexiest, cleverest, and funniest gal one could imagine, manna from Heaven.

How then could the void of Molly's emotional life be accounted for? Was she an un-person, or did there lie within her a beast slouching towards Bethlehem to be born? Her maternal grandfather was, by all accounts, a brutal, violent, philandering sailor, who returned periodically to beat his wife mercilessly, in the presence of their four children - a man who had an affair with that wife's best friend under her very nose, and who gave the family next to nothing on which to live. His mistress, in fact, often interceded by mail on their behalf, pleading with "Mr. McCarthy" to give the family more money, when she observed, or was told, that the children had outgrown their unsavory secondhand clothes and shoes, or as other needs arose. Molly's grandmother was, herself, thoroughly helpless and infantilized, subservient, beaten down... She referred to her violent husband only as "Mr. McCarthy ". "Mr. McCarthy is a good man," she would say, her eyes black and swollen, her face still freshly scarred.

The McCarthy's oldest daughter, Patty, ran away as soon as she was able to, and went to Hunter college on scholarship. She was either asexual or lesbian, no one was really sure. She was very bright, and possessed a great deal of general knowledge, but, sadly, was insufferably opinionated, a stubborn know-it-all, critical of everyone, especially Molly. The youngest daughter, Isabel, "Beefer", was obese, infantile, and much like her mother. She worked as a nanny and babysitter, and had endless, vain, pathetic crushes on various men, who, predictably and unfailingly, scorned her. "Beefy" was Mrs. McCarthy's favorite. Since Patty had nothing but contempt for her mother's weakness, that contempt translated into an equivalent loathing for her youngest sister, Isabel. The son, Brandon, was, by all accounts, schizophrenic, alcoholic, and a compulsive gambler. No one seemed to know or care if he were even alive anymore. He had, most probably, tried to rape Molly's mother, Julie, some 15 years ago. He had, at the very least, succeeded in breaking down the front door of Julie's apartment in an alcoholic rage. Julie and Patty were the only two siblings who communicated, although no one, including Julie, had ever seen Patty's apartment. This was never questioned or considered strange. Patty had a good job at Blue Cross, and was about to retire.

What can one say about Molly's mother, Julie? She grew up with a freewheeling attitude towards material things - a paradoxical reaction to the poverty of her youth, although she was also quite the pack rat, who saved everything, perhaps in response to her having lived both through the Depression and the hardships endured as a result of Mr. McCarthy's miserliness. She was understandably resentful of the rich Jewish girls with whom she attended summer camp, who made great fun of her secondhand clothes and torn shoes. She happily indoctrinated her children with a fairly mild, in the big picture, anti-Semitism.

The love of her life appeared in her thirties - a black short-order cook and self-proclaimed spiritual teacher, Herbie, who introduced her to every ridiculous, half-baked new-age notion concerning spirits, reincarnation, channeling, and other assorted nonsense that was in the air at the time. Apparently, he fucked like a machine which could go on forever, as if he were not even human - at least according to Julie. When he finally betrayed her, she had a very severe breakdown, hired a private investigator, and had her "bad" son, Brandon (inexplicably named after his delightful Uncle, mentioned earlier), find her a gun on the black market, with which she might kill Herbie and his new girlfriend. Years later, when her pain was more bearable, she incorporated the lost Herbie within herself through a gigantic conceptual cosmology based on his teachings. I believe the psychoanalytic fairy-stories refer to said process as "introjection", but it was obviously true in this case. She kept and keeps him alive and inside herself to this very day, frequently envisaging the various cosmically necessary conditions which insure that she and he will one day, in some world, be reunited. Although she remained sexually active for a while longer, no prior or more recent passion ever competed with Herbie. Her compassion and conscious priorities now focused almost exclusively on animals. The cry of a kitten touched her in a way no pain or misfortune of her own flesh and blood ever would. When she learned that her son, Brandon, had contracted HIV, she lectured him concerning his bad attitude, explaining, at ghastly length, how all illness is merely a product of mind. The loss of her beloved Yorkie, Muffy, however, unhinged her.

Clark, Molly's father, came from a traditional, Bible-toting, long-ago monied, but still self-consciously aristocratic Southern family, a family that had no intention of tolerating his homosexual "depravity", or the decadence of a big city. He was a weak man - pathetic, full of self-loathing, and hopelessly cowardly. And yet he was brave enough to leave the suffocating environment of his family, and of Southern "morality", to make his way to the big northern city of New York, where, possessing no particular skill, he began working as a waiter. Already alcoholic, he met Julie, who was desperate to get away from her own dysfunctional family. They engaged in at least one bisexual threesome, the stuff of legend, apparently, and married. At 19, Julie was pregnant with twins. Clark was horrified - this was his very worst nightmare. And yet, it must be noted - he stood by this young family, whether out of guilt or some sort of transplanted Southern notion of honor, it matters not. The environment in which Molly began to grow up was laced with poisonous cynicism, contempt, despair, and alcoholism. The marriage crumbled quickly and irrevocably, held together only by the bond of financial need. Clark would often walk by Molly's room late at night, when she was a girl, cursing the day she was born under his alcoholic breath. She would hide her head underneath the covers, sure that one day he would kill Julie. There was a confrontation between the two of them in the hall, with a knife… It was not spoken of.

Clark was a man someone outside the family might very well pity. Someone such as I. He had a certain sour dignity about him, perhaps the result of his brutal honesty and cynicism, and of his having stood by the family, coughing up much of his meager salary to support them, when he could have easily walked. He worked the graveyard shift at the Metropolitan Museum as a security guard by the time I met him, although I do recall Molly telling me, before I met him, that he was a curator at said institution - a man in very much voluntary, nocturnal contact with the dark and the sepulchral, shunning both day and other persons. He liked it that way. He mostly ignored his daughter, but once took Molly to the carousel at Central Park when she was around ten, after Julie had pleaded with him to do so. He asked her if she wanted a drink. He was trying to bond.

During Molly's youth, Julie worked nights at the telephone company. Her hysteria was monumental. She kept an enormous, vicious, neutered alley cat tied up in the kitchen, which wanted nothing more than to kill Molly, from the day she was born. Her brother, Brandon, ran away, like his mother and father, during his adolescence. He too, was a substance abuser and homosexual, like his father, although, unlike Dad, he was a troublemaker and far more aggressive. There was never a hint of discipline in the home, and he was acting out from very early on. Years of anonymous gay sex in the back of bookstores and park benches - drugs, robberies, fist and knife fights, guns - these were the script and stage props of Brandon's young life. He reportedly once threw Molly against the wall when she was an infant, and split her head wide open. His twin sister Alisa's promiscuity was legendary, in her own mind, at any rate, although anyone seeing her in her late thirties, as I did, would have had the same trouble as I believing that this loony, overweight, prematurely middle-aged woman was ever of any sexual or romantic interest to any remotely sentient being. She finally picked the perhaps most unappealing of her literally dozens of boyfriends to marry, and settled down with in South Jersey with this appallingly ignorant, alcoholic, lazy, and chauvinistic auto mechanic, whose name blessedly escapes me at the moment.

Molly looked, in this context, as if she were Wednesday Addams - a normal, well-adjusted foundling, left upon their family doorstep. (Well, there is this difference - the T.V. Addams family did love one another.) But looks can be deceiving. Molly herself always idealized the meditators and gurus, the more empty and dead their eyes the better - for what could be a better indication of enlightenment? Eyes were windows into the vast, seemingly untroubled emptiness within them, or so she believed.

She loved little boys, the beauty of their play and spontaneity, and wished, quite consciously, that she had been one, certainly from the onset of puberty, but most likely from quite a bit earlier on. This wish only grew more fervent as she was subjected, more and more, to her older sister's over-the-top slut shtick.

How did I come to love this woman? We skated over reality. I was, for a very long time, satisfied with that - with the most trivial of exchanges imaginable between two homo sapiens. I sometimes yearn for those days, even now - the numbness, the easy-come, easy-go childishness, the faux-domesticity. My blissful, domestic arrangement came at a rather over-inflated price, at the price of my self, my soul. I lived with someone who could neither nurture, nor even understand what it might mean to nurture or be nurtured - other than offering, or being offered, juvenile, cheerleader-level encouragement. Molly's folks told her that she was the product of a very much by chance, one night encounter, on a weekend, on which, coincidentally, Julie was not with her black boyfriend, and Clark, too, was alone - perhaps during one of those small windows of sexual quiescence in his life. I would imagine large quantities of alcohol were involved. A one-shot accident, she was born of two who violently loathed one another - locked, as they were, in a perpetual, suffocating, spiritually empty, financial and genetic dance/embrace, with nothing between them other than venomous contempt.

That Molly so much as walks the Earth, or that she is able to take pleasure in anything, ever, is a miracle. Her pursuit of quiet, hypnagogic states and intense physical activity is a triumph of creative self-medication, an endorphin-producing blessing for this poor, sad creature, for whom blessings have always been in conspicuously short supply.

I am reading the above in absolute disgust at the obscenely judgmental nature of its narrative. The overly-examined life is not worth living, and whose is more overly-examined than my own?

Oh my - this gal, this "Desiree", is very funny. And, dear Lord, her tits are nothing short of amazing.

December 9-11, 1995

Chapter 2

I never respected Molly. Hers was the most prosaic of minds - there was barely a nightlight on in that cavern, much less an occasional flash of lightning. It was muggy, humid, and stagnant from disuse. Neurons flapped in the occasional mild breeze with no discernible response from their neighbors. 'Twas a barren, desolate island, set apart from the world, and for all intents and purposes uninhabitable, an island upon which one would occasionally stumble upon hopelessly bitter, inedible Styrofoam fruit that, at first, looked inviting, and could pass for real from a distance, especially if one had been traveling, long-famished, on stormy seas, as I had.

But she was like my sister, right? Yes, of course, family. How could I resist her, this sister, this puss-infested fever blister. It is, perhaps, relevant that my own family are narcissistic swine, my parents, and one grandparent, at the very least - colossally undignified pains in the ass, of the sort whose little thoughts and little lives help stoke the hatred of Jews in the population at large. And then I ACTUALLY see them, those genetic baboons, those unwashed blabbermouths in the train stations, with their forty-seven kinder-vermin, their kippahs, black dresses, and wigs, their revolting, ill formed faces, with those slothful, bestial mouths - clutching wildly at their pear-shaped bodies, looking like they just arrived from some sewage-infested planet, thoroughly convinced of their superiority. Is it any wonder that the more aesthetically minded among us would, as often is not, trade their entire race for an invention of Bach?

My sister, Annie, may never have forgiven me for having had mental illness. I was, at least at one time, a source of embarrassment for her - I do believe that. So yes - perhaps Molly and I were like brother and sister. For Molly loved nothing more than to tease me, good-naturedly at times, and with a barbed viciousness at others. A form of intimacy? It can be. But it can be something quite other than that. Waiters would always assume that Molly was my sister the few times the three of us would go out. Annie told me she was gay years before she told either of our profoundly unintuitive parents. I was a psychological mess, but I believe I responded in the expected, sensitive, and politically correct way. I remember her saying "It hurt", after she had fucked some loser auto mechanic a few times, to see if being straight was even a remote possibility for her. I am not surprised that she picked the scum of the Earth to test the viability of heterosexuality in her life. I didn't go near a woman for three years after Katy died. And when I did, I intentionally chose one that was vile. Out of guilt? Because I deserved nothing more? Molly used to say it hurt as well. Well then - I imagine when it's smaller than a mousehole and dry as the Gaza strip, that would tend to be the deal, no? Every man's dream, right? Dry as graveyard dirt, with a tuft of desert moss. The first time I gave her an orgasm, she peed all over the mattress which lay on the floor in my pathetic little basement studio apartment. She was mortified, of course, and nothing remotely like that ever happened again. And, after that, orgasm for her was an infinitesimal nod, a not-even sneeze - as if she were out on a crisp autumn day and were to remark on the chilliness of the weather with the tiniest of shivers - momentary and close to unnoticeable. For, truth be told, she was mortified by the very fact that she was a woman. "Don't bang me", she'd frequently say. There would be deafening silence, accompanied by a passion more or less equivalent to that of a repressed schoolboy being raped by his lecherous headmaster. How I decided that this was an acceptable situation is hard to say. I think I can safely say that, for one thing, as a result, I started becoming interested in pornography. At least women could PRETEND to be enthusiastic, even if, when the cameras were off them, they would start in to weep, and/or scream, "Get this cum out of my fucking hair!" Or - "I can't fuck this creep without a helluva lot more coke than this, Rocco!"

Both shared the same loathing of men, at the very same time that they would have both liked to have been male. Perhaps it's more of the latter than the former. They both had contempt for their fathers - the one overt, the other covert. Molly feigned pity and would have had you believe she was understanding of her family's flaws - she feigned compassion and pity for all mankind, as well, but it was only a pose. She despised people. People had made her suffer and feel inadequate, since her very first days on Earth. She must have rejoiced when her father finally killed himself - this was the hateful monster whom she had always feared would kill her Mommy - the man who, when she was a child, walked by her bedroom in the dead of night, in a drunken stupor, cursing her, and wishing that she had never been born. A part of her must have been screaming - "Die, you ancient, sickly, faggot loser! Die for what you did to me!"

Molly was horrified by pornography in the most prudish and absurd of ways - "Look at those men banging those poor women, shoving their cocks in their mouths." Did her father fuck her? Did her father stick his most likely tiny alcoholic cock in her, at some point? Did he stick it in his own son, the second generation, self-loathing fag? The former is quite unlikely, since women were not his cup of tea, for the most part. The latter - who knows? Her mother dug it, that's for sure, when Herbie would stick his big, black dick in her, while Molly, with whom she shared a room, was forced to pretend she was asleep. When she wasn't stepping gingerly to avoid being mauled by the vicious alley cat in the hall on the way to the bathroom, that is. These things can do a number on you - one doesn't need a Freud to explain why. "It hurts! You're too big! Go slower!" To which I would respond, in my mind at least - "You don't want me to slide a pillow under your ass? Is that just a tad too daring for your, I suppose understandable, Victorian worldview, given what you endured as a kid? You must have seen Herbie, or Sonny, or etc., etc., slide plenty of pillows under your mom's ass, no? You're going to now pretend that you're offended by carnality? You? Who sucked many a cock as a teenager, sometimes absolute strangers' cocks, after they had barfed up some inarticulate piece of disingenuous, adolescent flattery? You opened your mouth wide to articulate your gratitude to them, in the only way you were able to do so, given that you have the vocabulary of a toddler. And yet you still kept that little pussy of yours glued shut. You had anal sex with three guys out on some sleazy fake yacht in the middle of the ocean, and now I can't slide a pillow under your ass?" I came inside of Molly probably a half-dozen times in close to ten years. In the meantime, we would jerk each other off like children, after listlessly fucking like it didn't matter very much. At least that part was honest - it didn't. "Can't you make some goddamn noise? Are you suppressing the need to sneeze? Oh, I see... That's your orgasm!"

And so we jerked each other off, literally and metaphorically, for a very long time. She couldn't wear a diaphragm, for reasons her subconscious made no offer or effort to share with her. For foreplay, she would stand in the bathroom, in front of the mirror, examining herself under a microscope, scrutinizing her acne scars, often for upwards of an hour and a half. All the cleaning, and picking, and obsessing in the world couldn't change the fact that she was only a somewhat better than average-looking person, with monumental psychological baggage, and that she appeared and functioned as if she had been emotionally lobotomized (she had been, in a protracted self-surgery), sublimating all that terribly annoying human stuff, all the difficult feelings of anger, loss, and love, along with all that other unsavory, regrettable shit that contributes to our personhood, into the quicksand of her trivial compulsions and defenses.

Molly would plop herself down in bed with a repulsive mud mask on, in a nightgown fit for a seventy-year-old mental patient. She would then start to read running magazines, or squealing endless "Om"s - the latter providing forgivable inspiration for homicide, take it from me. Anything to kill the remotest possibility of passion. She went to great lengths to stay out of touch with her sexual self, and, luckily, for the most part, at any rate, took care to stay out of touch with her ugly, vindictive self - that vile, satanic creature that had long ago set up shop in her unlovely skull with the ferocity and sadism of a spurned supernatural being. Was I crazy, or did she start getting a little wet those last couple of months? She said my affair had made me a better lover - which suggests to me only that the cock which was now in her had been in someone else not too long ago, and that the thought of this excited her.

I had a great deal of trouble touching her during the affair. I couldn't even really look at her. Half racked with guilt, but at least half overwhelmed with repulsion, a repulsion which had a new, demonic clarity. I was beginning to loathe her. I had and have a grudging appreciation for just how hard her life had been, i.e., "Poor Molly - her defenses were necessary, a remarkable testament to the human will to survive. Just remember and consider, if only for a moment, the sordid, pathological family structure in which she was forced to grow up - 'tis a wonder she survived at all!" At the same time, I still despised her for being so damaged, for being such a quasi-human, such a shadow of a person. It's awful for one to be unable to allow something one knows perfectly well, irrefutably and rationally, to squash one's hateful, unfairly judgmental feelings. And now I resented Desiree, as well, simply for throwing her into such irrevocably, well-lit relief.

"You simpleton, you tin-woman, you stubborn, condescending, patronizing, self-loathing, misfit loser. I spent ten years of my life with you, and I fucking hate myself for it." I can still hear that little voice in my head, attempting to scream, from the very first date - "Get away, don't do this!" And meeting Julie and Clark supported, unequivocally, every negative notion I had of her; the apple - squashed, rancid, worm and razor blade-infested - tends to fall not too far from the corrupted and tainted tree.

Molly's Mom professed to being susceptible to the charms and passions of men who were into music, or created it - of seeming to be moved by them - but then, she is such a disingenuous, Pollyanna phony, who's really to know? Perhaps she's just another Molly-machine, whose workings are just harder to glean, because the volume has been turned up to eleven. Her Dad was not moved by anything - not by beauty, not by his children... Perhaps by fond memories of booze, by moving his bowels, by walking up the stairs without tripping, by successfully finding his earplugs, eye mask, and sleeping pills... These things likely provided him with the motivation to struggle through another few hours on this godawful planet.

"Cut the cord," she used to say - constantly, referring with pride to the way in which she had never had any long-lived attachments - how no friend, boyfriend, or human influence of any kind had remained to play any further part in her life, once their specified time upon the stage in her little, self-directed play sans any real narrative had run its course. Who are those who "cut the cord ", if not those who have never bonded with anyone in the first place? She needn't have cut it - there was no cord, there was no place on her, or in her, where one might attach a cord. She was as smooth as a marble statue - what was desiccated and leprous was all inside, yet somehow managed to survive next to a soul made of ice.

We slept through 10 years in a prison-crib - I and she, my sister, my despot-enemy, my butch-mannequin. Would it have been better had she never been born, as her father often wished? It would have been better for me had I not, that I have known since my consciousness first turned on like a horrified, two-bit Walmart nightlight. Would the world have missed her? With no cords to bind her to Earth, she might have floated freely into space, the vacuum of space, where nothing could have hurt or grabbed hold of her. What kind of relationship had we had, that she could be supportive and unconflicted about my affair? Psycho-sister, qu-est-ce sais?

My prostate blew up like a softball. I couldn't ejaculate. A few dozen more muscles, and some effective drugs to get over my hopeless self-consciousness, and I could've been a damned porn star. Her non-presence was satanic. A she-devil's ritual of mutual masturbation, dreamily narcotized. Elizabeth Bathory in the body of a 24-year-old Shirley Temple. The only time her eyes twinkled with even a hint affection for me was when she would look at my baby pictures. What did she want with that little boy? To what unconscious sadism would she have subjected him, had she been his Mommy? Empty life, empty promises, deceitful, mouthed-only inferences of our BOND, our implied, eternal BOND - our family, our dogs - LIES! LIES! LIES! Mephistopheles, thou. Wouldst I were Faust.

Hi, this is my girlfriend! She has no intellectual interests, thoughts, creativity, curiosity, sexual passion, or enthusiasms for anything besides her running (and that simply because it comes easily to her, and is a balm for her ravaged self-esteem - not out of any objectively measurable love for the sport, not because she wishes to excel - no, no, no - nothing like that - simply because she's fairly good at it without trying - to try would then compel her to feel she had to be good, because, of course, she would be "trying" - I, above and beyond most people, understand such reluctance, ugh). She is ill-spoken, and has little or no general knowledge - hence one is likely to find it frightful trying to have any sort of conversation with her.

I had a supreme sense of entitlement, the curse of Le Petit Jew-Prince - vile, despicable wretch that I am. But I was the one who had to live with this fucking shell of a person, right? So I eventually decided to do whatever the fuck I wanted, with no shudders of conscience, no self-congratulatory moralizing. I'm an artistic, sensitive guy, and my emotional susceptibility and temper excuses me, needless to say! - from having to worry about others' potentially hurt feelings. Dear God, what a prick I am. But, as she told me time and time again, her feelings were not hurt. As the son of a violently abusive mother, I pride myself on my intuition, hunches, and ability to read others, my ability to scan the smallest oscillations in their inflections, demeanors, and voices for signals and cues, to know how an insignificant facial tick might signal some volcanic emotion, hidden even from themselves, which might turn vicious on a dime. Actually, I don't "pride myself" at all about this - it's what any ferret or squirrel would be forced to learn, were it to grow up in analogous circumstances.

I got no sense whatsoever that what Molly said about not having been hurt was anything other than the truth. No sense that, beneath her affectless encouragement, lay the jealous rage of a scorned woman - that, not far beneath those superficial reassurances was a bile-spewing fiend. With fiends like that, who needs enemas? I just inferred she did not love me in any way which was recognizable to me as love. I inferred this from my own massive experience, ever so mature and world-weary as it was. Hahaha, no.

The first night I slept at Desiree's, I writhed the whole sleepless night on a bed of self-lacerating guilt. I met Molly at one of her dopey races the next morning. She cheerfully and mindlessly accepted my far less than convincing, halfhearted lies.

I finally admitted my guilt one morning, after I'd spied Molly, with our two dogs, as I disembarked from the Long Island Railroad after another adulterous tryst. Why she was there, precisely then, at 8:30 AM, I am not sure. It was as if she were waiting for me - perhaps horribly worried, perhaps furious, perhaps heartbroken, perhaps all three - except that, in her face, there was nothing to suggest any of that. There was no affect there, at all.

I could no longer lie, at least to the extent I had been up until that point. I fixed my most intense and analytic gaze upon her face, rapt with attentiveness, hungry for any clue which might suggest what she was feeling. I told her I had slept with Desiree, but just once, that it had only represented a bit of warmth between friends, blah, blah, blah - on and on with the malarkey and fictions.

She didn't flinch, although she was curious. She seemed supportive, even empowering. "Oh... How was it?" she said, blankly. My jaw dropped. I had wished so deeply for her not to be hurt by this, but that all paled in comparison to my hurt feelings, which eventually morphed into rage, at her non-reaction. What was I to her, anyway?

Desiree and I spoke the same language - the language of a once-intellectual European Jewry - a delightful (or sickening, depending on your point of view) mishmash of angst, narcissism, self-lacerating humor, and clever witticisms. She was a godsend.

Whenever I was able to see my machinations in any modestly objective light, e.g., my endless phone calls with Desiree on that fateful trip to Seattle, I judged my behavior to be beyond despicable, unforgivably so. I was a bastard, there was no denying it. (Although that would mean, thank God, that those two horrid people weren't my real parents - that, at least, would be a relief.)

There are times, even now, when I wake up in a sweat - missing her, aching for her, mourning the lost tranquility and bliss of our "home". There is a part of me, a very large part of me, that still loves her, that will always love her. She is a good, kind, and loving person, who had been subjected to godawful stressors and abuse. One morning, I called her at work, only to hear her babbling in a characteristically judgmental, condescending tone to one of her unfortunately less experienced colleagues. How quickly I had forgotten - how quick I had been to idealize! The woman was and remains a moron, so there is always that bottom line - one of many. Throwing her out the door was perhaps the most liberating of opportunities the universe has ever offered me. For, in so doing, I flung the portals of my own, self-created dungeon wide open. Or did I? Would I not take her back, in a heartbeat? Whether I would live now or die, whether I would be greeted with the smell of lilacs or that of rotting corpses, I would, at least for a time, walk with my eyes and ears open. So I told myself.

January 15-17, 1996

Monarch notes

Music is a holy art
Of solace, depth, and mystery -
But it never changes anything -
It's bound and restricted by history.

Folks call Mozart an Earthly prince -
Some claim he was a God!
But if you had told Machiavelli that,
He'd have thought it rather odd.

Drammi giocosi, murderous Asians -
Requiem Masses, Mongol invasions -
Don Giovanni comes off a bit wan
Next to the conquests of Genghis Khan.

No Regrets

The house is burning down.
The rats smell it from miles away.
The groundhog next door ambles over.
He's up a bit later than usual, roasting marshmallows.
The birds rejoice.
The earth trembles, chuckles contemptuously, pisses itself, then
sleeps the sleep of death - the sleep of a peace unknown to me,
unknown to all men.

Regret?
Only that I wasn't there, as comatose as a near-lethally-drunken
pig, and waking up to an unimaginable, yet still welcome, Hell.
Extending my hand to Dante, as he understandably recoils.
One wishes to be charred to a fine powder of ash, to disappear
in mist, to finally bound through those absurd, Cheshire-Cat-like
holes in the bedroom wall, which intermittently appeared, like a
farrago of viragos from the beyond.
Promises of an oblivion where no famished, ravenous ghosts
await.

There was that girl -
What was her name?
I don't know.
Does it matter?
Aren't they more or less the same, at the close of the play?
Gigantic, oozing honeypots at the center of the galaxy,
pretending to be this one, that one - the innocent schoolgirl, the
jaded, played-out whore, the latest false Messiah?
The latter, who, with dulcet tones, shrieks ecstatic as she pins
you, wriggling like an insect, in her collection, which she reviles,
and which she's already forgotten?
Which was borrowed in the first place, from a long-forgotten
wordsmith.
I would tell you what his name was, if I could.

Yes, she was beautiful.
But then I was, as well.
The world was still green and wildly pulsing -
Every cloud rained possibility.
"Do you think I'm gay?" I asked, as I was banging the shit out of her.
"No, sweetheart. I'm quite sure you're not," she said, giggling hysterically.
It was the time of our lives, a time of blanketed, blissful stupidity.
When the sun wasn't busy warming everyone and everything from the inside out, the moon beamed the purest inspiration, and sang sweet, impossibly intoxicating songs.
That was before they arrived - the adults, with their grimaces, their lies, their dead eyes.
Before she and I became one of them.
Corpses of children, doomed to remember.
Entombed.
Yes, she was a fool.
But I was, too.
And what is more wonderful than to be beautiful and foolish, to awaken, untroubled, unaware that rabid hyenas are biding their time, waiting to drag you off to Hell?
Listen...
You can hear them slobbering, their slop salivating in the ether, in rabid anticipation.

And so it was that the cellist, the goddess, the most beautiful woman who ever looked twice at me, who I now realized was, and is, a pea-brained, unconscious fraction of a person, threw me over.
Better for her, lucky for me.
She said she still loved me.
Laughable, really.
So I drove, and drove, and drove till the night turned a deep shit brown, and my eyes began to bleed - till I slept behind the wheel God knows where - after having looked, impotently, for a railroad track to lie down upon, to find release - and finding only potholes, and tattooed waitresses with 4000-year old bags under their eyes - in squalid diners in lowlife Mick slums of Boston.

Contempt in the faces of every haggard morning commuter and squirrel, vultures razzing me from every tree on every block…
Perhaps it wasn't contempt, after all, just boring, old, predictable Death.
The dead place - where adults live.
Where I now found myself.

I coulda been a contender.
Ya, a contender.
Fer sure.
Faw shizzle.
As it stands, my status as a monumental underachiever will, at least, be good for an epic laugh.
A short story written by another world-class underachiever, who works in a sweltering hot factory under another, who answers to a third.
Who wouldn't?
Who wouldn't laugh?
I'll laugh.
St. Peter will laugh, as he pisses on me, and tells me to take a left at the dark woods, sit underneath a willow weeping, with bitter sap in my eyes, and wait for Virgil, Godot, love - all the crap I thought had been promised me.
Just wait -
Your life will start.
Any day now.
Just clench your chattering teeth, and count to ten.
Meditate.
Yes, do be mindful.

A person can hurt back.
There's a certain dark nobility in it.
You can never hurt the right ones though - the bigs, the ones who towered over you - the ones who beat you with drawers, made you touch their filthy cunts, made you want to puke your life down their throats, down to the depths, and up to the non-existent heavens.

Yes - then came the others.

But I was already dead, this was all the purest, posthumous activity.

Posthumous I love you's, posthumous fucking, posthumous music, emanating from mausoleums I hadn't the nerve to enter.

What was her name   Violet?

The gorgeous Italian gal with the big tits, who said she loved me?

Whom I lay next to, and melted into as if she were das ewig Weibliche, the Ur-Woman, she who stood for all the others?

The one whose warm body could make me tingle like I had finally, once and for all, left myself behind, left everything in this world behind - standing, no, floating, on the gentle tide of a delicious oblivion?

A mirage. All a mirage.

A puppet, operated by a dark, smirking God - like all the other mirages.

As memory turns to cinders, does she burn as well?

Is she screaming now, as I purge myself of her and all the others?

It is sweet, it is bitter - it is my life.

As for phony ID's, I hardly need a formal one.

I've been inhabiting this body from afar for decades.

It's not me you see, my dear.

It's only a phantom.

I've long since gone.

I still fear -

I fear pain, but even that fear is dwindling to the same cinders my idiot body is becoming.

The world is quieter, dimmer, more forgiving - ever dumber and more meaningless.

You call me by my name.

My name is nothing.

This thing that throbs and thrives in me has no name, has never had, and will never have, a name.

The whistle of the train in the distance.

My deliverance.

The casting off of the ragged body.

The salvation of the ragamuffin soul on a distant shore.

I know these streets.
I've walked them countless times, looking for her.
Time is a bubbly froth -
One need only dive in headfirst, cast off one's self, and call her name.
If she had ears to hear.
But there are no ears here, no eyes, no hearts.
It's a death march through a frozen, uncaring universe.
I could get used to this.
I could build a house of glass here.
To house my heart of glass.
This is a neighborhood to which one could grow accustomed, in which one could comfortably retire.

But there they are, once again, the stragglers, the living, the ones who always want something from you.
Yelling at you to stay, just a bit more - yanking you from oblivion into the cold glare of a cheesy interrogation room, staffed by brutal, sadistic, two-bit actors.
I have no happy place to go to.
Only this place - this place of filth, need, and ugliness.
Filled with rotting flesh and false protestations of love.

They say they "need" me.
As if I could fill the gaping wound that bleeds from the base of their spine through their petty, grasping hearts and empty heads.
The ones they're utterly unaware of.
Ha.
There was a time I allowed myself to drown in that selfsame need.
To believe it, to embrace it, to live for THEM.
Come back to us, come back from oblivion!
        <dry echoes in a field of dead wheat, under a sick sun>
Needy wives, children, animals, friends, students, the liars who say they loved you, that they still love you.

I am floating, floating in a warm bath of honey, arsenic, and ether.
I look down on the burning house and smile, as my ancient, alcohol-drenched body throws off a lovely light, for that one brief, ecstatic moment.
For that moment, the world is beautiful, and full of meaning.
But I turn away, because I both wish to and must, to quench what is left of my soul's thirst in an avalanche of grief, of passion, of self-conscious, scripted, deeply corny farewells.
I look down at one, last, surprising-for-an-old-guy hard-on, made only the more absurd and hilarious because of its meaninglessness, and am swallowed...
Me, my life, all my stupid, pointless regrets - in a delicious blaze of ecstatic madness.

Philistine Sally and Pheromone Sue

Philistine Sally and Pheromone Sue
Played hooky from high school and went to the zoo -
The former got pelted by simian poo,
While the latter went down on a guy in the loo.

Once they were home and their visit was through,
Sally just sat in the juice of her stew -
But Sue made quite certain her friends that were true
Knew who Sue blew in the loo of the zoo.

Postcards from the Abyss
a/k/a History of Us

The mountain stood, gentle against the sky, enveloped in wisps of cloud, like a fetus, peacefully strangled in its own placenta. There was a time when its hills and cliffs were vibrant with roads and the bustle of traffic - perfumed seductions from a warm future. Now they lie congealed - spidery varicose veins on a rotting woman's corpse, incubating a bustling, furry, pubic undergrowth in which I am quite lost - wandering, posthumous, invisible.

In a world where homesick, misanthropic stewardesses serve Bloody Marys to blond athletes, imbecilic, and dewy-eyed, on long unexamined jets, destined to crash momentarily into soot black seas; where young girls dye their hair purple, pierce their tongues, and let mindless high-school boys fuck them, to torture their Mums, impress their peers, and convince themselves they are alive, nay, that they even wish to be alive - there is a small still place, hidden beneath the crashing surf, and in between the echoes of a thousand meaningless, barely attended, and fast forgotten conversations. I can't take you there. No one can. Shhh... Listen...

I had a great-grandfather, once sun-drenched and bursting full of sap, the rapturous poetry of ravenous sweat and bulging desire pumping his green veins. Can you hear his heart pounding, as he awakens in a violent seizure of dread and longing, convinced he is about to fall through the creaky, wooden floor of his filthy hovel, into the silent abyss of the airless night? Soon enough, he was sawdust, charnel soot, his once vibrant pulp bubbling and hissing on the walls of the ancient crematorium, digested by clouds, and pissed by future rains on his children's children. Shh... A baby is crying. Who can remember being fern, stalk, and lizard, but a few moments ago?

There is a message, just over the horizon, beyond the windswept lake where the fat ladies lie, sneaking furtive, greedy glances at the bronzed and muscled life-guards.

When one is sufficiently dehydrated, the surface of the eyeball acts as a powerful and mucus-filled glue, which fuses the eye and lid. One must then manually alternate the position of the lid, closing the eye when the burning sensation becomes intolerable, and opening it again when sight is either desirable or becomes essential. A ferocious inwardness, to which certain ancient cultures ascribed transcendent spiritual qualities, is thus attained. If one is able to sufficiently objectify this pain, to dissociate one's "self" from it, the need to frantically open and shut the eye subsides. The eyeball itself then becomes infected, growing gradually rigid, and sinking deeper and deeper into its socket. Paradoxically, one's "second sight" blossoms into a luxurious, intoxicating opulence.

Job is an OK book, if your cup of tea is a murderous, psychopathic God who revels in His egomaniacal, grandiose bluster, and who offers not a hint of solace - personally, I prefer Ecclesiastes. I relate to the pomposity, and narcissistic apathy concerning the suffering of others one finds in the former, but aspire to the world-weary, bird's-eye view of the latter. Would that there were some bird, perhaps some black as filth raven, infinitely large and powerful, upon whom I could hitch a ride to a nearby black-hole, bubbling and ravenous, gobbling up the dying galaxy which surrounds it, and stopping only for the occasional belch or briefest of naps, into which I could dive. Vanish. Forget. As if I never had been. My fondest wish. Cancel that. A blond spilling out of her halter top just walked by, pouting. I'll stay for the movie after all.

The eyes of new fathers follow the paths of their young children, scouting for potential danger, yet never failing to furtively check if you, too, are equally entranced by their magnificent progeny. In the locker room, they admire their own genitals in much the same way - a hormone-driven, fugue state of delighted disbelief, pride, and befuddled bravado. And the child - that greedy little Frankenstein, from whose neck nature has graciously deigned to remove the bolts, in order that other hopeless, momentarily fertile blockheads might be hoodwinked into the very same, cosmic, hopelessly overpriced Kentucky Derby of decay and death - note how the thing drinks in experience indiscriminately, happily masticating on both a canvas of Caravaggio and the lead-filled paint chips on the floor with the same voracious gusto.

An old man is an aged wine, whether subtle and fine, or loathsomely bitter, a decaying piece of wooden sculpture, whose bark has been whittled away by wisdom, weather, and worms - a burnished etching of Dürer, a chaotic, incoherent piece of disease-bearing driftwood, which the sea has nonchalantly belched upon the beach. What he is, or was - these things matter not to the maggots who devour his entrails, and deposit his eviscerated carcass on the crisp, fresh January snow.

Roads that lead nowhere are extraordinarily well-paved, traveled, and maintained. They routinely double back, actively reinserting themselves into the ongoing hurly-burly like a well-oiled, heat-seeking enema.

A foolish old man with a wide-brimmed hat trips over a mole's den, awakening an incandescently blue woman's head and torso from the earth. As soon as she begins her insufferably pretentious, endless pontifications, concerning the warp and woof of our mercy-starved world, he stuffs her yammering mouth full of dirt and boulders, in a fit of wild fury. God occasionally whispers to Man, but His mouth is always full of stale, cheap, five and dime store crackers.

When I was a boy, I held a match near the head of a tiny helpless turtle, in an attempt to make him feel the rib-crushing, suffocating horror that I felt, bottled up as I was in a vice-like straitjacket, and thrown into a world spinning wildly out of my control. I'll never forget his lacerating gaze of all-knowing anger, stuffed full to bursting with the ennui of a billion successive incarnations. That furious little homunculus was me, was you, was all of us - and we have all - you, I, he - seen it all, countless times, in scene after scene of inexhaustible absurdity - everything, over and over again. If only we could remember.

In medieval Thailand, female adulterers were routinely dismembered, and then fed to members of the clergy, in intricately carved rice bowls, during highly stylized ceremonies. When one of the emperor's concubines was found with a member of the court, even a eunuch, the two were strapped to a fiercely barbed spit, rotating over a roaring charnel house fire, and forced to gag on one another's genitalia. Ceremonial scarves muffled the screams from their parched, stuffed throats, as the flames gradually consumed them. If a concubine was found in the embrace of another concubine, the punishment was somewhat less ghoulish, but no less deadly. Bound naked, mouth to crotch, in the city square, under heavy guard, and with the incessant jeering of the townsfolk pummeling their braincases like shrapnel, they were left for days, and sometimes weeks, to gradually starve to death.

As radio wave-borne images of cute kitty videos careen out into galaxies fifty light-years from our lonely, desolate, mindlessly spinning earth, as the boys we once knew come, more and more, to resemble wizened, post-menopausal grandmothers, as the parks, where we once bubbled over like the froth of fresh champagne, sparkling under a seemingly new and honeyed sun, are paved over, and crushed to a thin crust of forgetting, what remains for us? Who are we then, now? When the only measure of time's passing is each day's baffling, surreal strangeness? I saw an elderly gentleman skydive by my cabin window, fretfully ripping the innards out of an old spring-loaded clock, cursing all the while - God, fate, the Buddha, his vile spouse, his ungrateful, spoiled children, and everyone else who couldn't be bothered any longer to notice or listen to him.

During the Inquisition, persons with tapeworms in their guts were starved for many many days. The Inquisitor would then jamb a sugar-encrusted crucifix down their throats, replete with an infinitely detailed rendering of the suffering, lacerated Christ. When the worm finally emerged to encircle the cross, in a drunken, ecstatic bacchanal of insatiable filth, it was delicately disentangled, flayed alive, dyed the deepest purple, and entombed, for all eternity, in a meticulously constructed stained-glass image of the temptation in Eden. The sufferer's throat was then slit, his carcass gutted, the entrails cremated, and poured into a box of tin, upon which had been placed many zealous and earnest curses by many zealous and earnest monks, which was eventually buried in unhallowed ground.

In mathematics, there is a class of functions so transcendentally beautiful, that those few and privileged beings, who begin to fathom their implications, gradually lose all interest in the outside world - to such an extent that they eventually become content to nourish their brains and nervous systems with their own muscles, sinews, internal organs, and, finally, bones. The holy sacrament continues until such time as they lie completely helpless and emaciated, a mass of violently twitching, pulpy-wet neurons, upon which a pair of raw, pulsating stalks blossom into bloodshot-weary, hypertrophic eyes, beatifically sedate and heavy-lidded.

It is said that in one of the lesser known byways of the inferno, Pete Seeger sings eternally indistinguishable chestnuts of American folksong as, all the while, rotting, cancerous nodes gradually encircle, inflame, and finally sever his vocal cords one from the other. This process repeats itself in perpetuity. Garrison Keillor is, needless to say, master of ceremonies. The applause is deafening. It is, after all, a human interest story.

There was a train that used to pass by my house, just before dawn. No matter where I was, or what the position of my body, it would pass just behind me, a bit elevated, and to my left. No one else ever heard it, which, to me, proved its existence beyond any shadow of doubt. On any given night it might be carrying Polish Jews on their way to Dachau, goats with red slits for eyes, piled high and suffocating atop one another, gouging each other's flesh, and praying goat-prayers for the sweetness of a swift oblivion, carloads of moronically babbling nouveau riche, swollen with food, liquor, and unearned wealth, returning to their multi-terraced, underwater stucco dwellings, proudly exchanging photos and anecdotes of their gilled, pampered, and fish-tailed children, refugee Rwandan women, screaming in pain and clutching wildly at the doors and windows, in hopeless attempts to escape, pregnant to bursting with their famished, already toothed unborn - and my father, reading, with his legs up, happy-deaf to my pleas and shrieks, as I ran alongside, wildly panting, with my heart violently pounding. If you see him, do let him know how hard I tried to reach him, how very hard, only to find that his heart had burst into flames long ago, his ears and mind eaten away by worms.

There were times when I would flinch wildly, causing the train to disengage from its tracks, and sail through the endless vacuum of space. I would then become aware of a goat-hoofed stranger - well, at first a stranger, now, perhaps, a friend - sitting comfortably and patiently at the right foot of my bed, as I lay there paralyzed in milky-monstrous sleep, waiting, dreading... who had been there since the very beginning, before I was even a twinkle in my wretched parents' gangrenous eyes, noting my progress from bud, to bloom, to bulbous concupiscence, taking careful note of the ever-growing stench of decay which surrounded me, waking, sleeping, fleeing, it mattered not. A farmer, a fisher, a fisher of men, the one for whom days and years, centuries and eons, mean nothing. His shroud was draped long and low, comforting in the way only terror can be comforting, terror I well knew was there all along, right behind that all too familiar fold, there in the fabric of space-time, into which I would sometimes fall soundlessly, into that fiendish, crumb-filled pants pocket, in which long dormant, gaping maws shred the living, randomly and mindlessly, in their forever dreamless sleep. There was nothing grand or theatrical about it - no monolith slabs, no games of chess, tunnels of soothing white light, or honeyed affirmations of the dearly departed. Quite bureaucratic, really. Clinical. The same old tale Beelzebub has been telling his grandchildren since the Big Bang, endlessly regurgitated and recycled - calm, without affect, signifying nothing. He is stupendously bored, truth to tell, the old fellow, but needs must engage in the telling once more, for, if he doesn't, he too would be liable to be shred to bits by older Gods and Furies of whom even he is horror-struck.

As a child I used to leave the closet door sometimes open, sometimes closed - to either be aware of his coming, or in a feeble attempt to bar his entry. I suppose I was at least sometimes successful, for, at times, I slept soundly through his relentless and inevitable visits, soothed by sham defenses, and the nearness of two who promised my eternal protection. That they did, during waking hours. Come the gloom of midnight, and, suddenly, there they were again, masks off, joined with him, in a witches' sabbath of violence and gleeful sadism. One has joined hell's ranks, the other clings to a cliff by a bitten, broken-off fingernail.

They were the white noise purporting to insulate my child-sleep against the jingle-jangle morning of the devil's sanitation crew. And they were that crew, as well, proud to be in the very most front ranks of its demons, amongst its most fervently ambitious perpetrators.

How I miss the old underground brothel. It's a shame the feds smoked the mob out of what was, for them, such an uncharacteristically creative business. I remember the cranky, painted crone who stood like a sentinel at the tunnel's entrance, with an absurdly self-important seriousness, as if she were collecting tickets at some exquisitely renovated Baroque church, for a performance by the Tallis Scholars of Josquin and Palestrina. An elementary school cafeteria lady, surely, who had been picked up, wriggling and screaming, in the talons of a rapacious pterodactyl, dipped in a hot, bloody river of yellow piss venom and Salisbury steak gravy, and deposited, along with thousands of other indistinguishable, eviscerated, elementary school cafeteria workers in this hellish, Madame Tussaud's hall of mirrors. Directly behind her, a large, and overly-lit room, in which enormous silicon-enhanced breasts hung from hideous, ancient heads, heads with red-rimmed, exhausted eyes and disfigured collagen lips, looking as if they had been stuck on by a blind, drunken potter, mouths which hawked caged sideshow hookers, large swaths of whose skin hung from garden stakes - women with bloody, lidless eyes where nipples ought to have been, the mouths on their violently stretched face masks attempting to violently drown one another out with their snarled, grunted offers of vigorous fellatio, all the while navigating through a room strewn full of random sacks of ancient hag-titties, and severed limbs of long gone great-aunts pulsating, gesticulating in wild proto-flesh-speak. A real man ought to have been able to enjoy himself there. Were I a real man, I could most certainly have enjoyed myself here, had I not been forced, by something broken within me, to slink off - craven, defeated and having spent nothing of myself. A real man would not invariably begin to obsess how they and he were made mostly of empty space, and become suddenly, hopelessly paralyzed with the fear of falling into the infinite vacuum which was rapidly opening up just beneath him. Can you see them in the hall there, the ghoulish vampires with their razor-sharp nails, whispering, smirking, waiting for the carefree athletes and sailors? I remember, on each occasion, looking desperately for an exit. There was, invariably, only one - a whip-vicious, violently lurching log-flume ride, in which one squirmed, desperately nauseated, like a boneless mouse, clutching one's torn, bloodied ears in an attempt to avoid their deadly, narcotic, repulsive yet infinitely seductive sirens' song, wafting down, like poisonous incense, from above.

At the library, there are drafty catacombs, lined with the dead and cast-off skins of still molting cultures. Long ago, I rubbed myself eagerly against those delicious, velvety casket linings, so full of solace, and the promise they would somehow protect me from the horrors and cataclysms which lurked outside. Oh, to experience again that first flush of my easy, effortless immortality - to be encased in the milky-white bosom of my flawless infant skin, encased in the inexhaustible milky white bosom of sweet, dream-filled nights spent removing from that still pristine skin the dried newsprint of presumed eternal profundities - before that skin turned leprous, before the once bejeweled stars of my youth grew faint, before my once lean, rapacious body came to feel so appallingly strange, before it came to eventually denounce me. When a man's brain has been stuffed, once too often, full of the petty ruminations of tyrannical ancestors, only then does one come to betray himself, and what he might have been, or might have kept on being, sufficiently to become a philosopher, to bid adieu to the land of the living, to choke to death, to drown, hopelessly affixed to the head of a pin, surrounded by incessantly garrulous blowhards screaming endless filth and nonsense, from their abyss into what has now become one's own.

<Oh, you men who think or say that I am malevolent, or misanthropic, how greatly do you wrong me.> I am no easily dismissed, black-as-pitch class clown, buried to the neck in a quicksand of self, burbling stale, exasperating witticisms. You would have me gentle, nourishing others, like fresh rain and Japanese gardens, full of grace and humility. Fools and blind men all. I will feed and clothe you, only to stab your fat and stylishly bedecked guts

to the quick, spilling what was left, of and in you, to the ground, as you watch helplessly, and stupendously betrayed. I am that, but much else besides. I will spin your skin anew, on a loom made of galaxies, into fingers which reach, tendril-like and delicate, into the endless abyss of everything and nothing, wildly flailing and thrashing about in the desperate hope of a familiar touch or sensation. I will wind your starry fingers through my own, until the powdered universe binds and fuses us into a single filament, and rains down a honeyed forgetting, which will course, delicious and sensuous, through our infinitely supple, once-again-infant veins.

Look, listen, feel...

We are, for this infinitely brief, ecstatically astonished moment, and, hence, for all eternity, born again...

racked with sorrow, rapt in care...
("rapt", i.e., spoken rapidly and rhythmically)

on a staircase drenched in poison in a house that's not a home a mausoleum and museum where sarcophagi have hammers strings and keys from which one flees there stands a wraith who has been hobbled and whose hips are not quite working in the ways she might have wanted as she lectures to a crowd that's filled with flashbacks of the gods they used to worship who are crazed in their impatience with the cruelty of the living hence they dream up pointless cakewalks which are danced by mortal puppets who are dangled from a rope not made of velvet spun by zombies in the back rooms and the loos of bombed-out coal bins lit with candles on the wane as they complain about their roommates who don't follow all the rules that they have laid out for the chess games with their rivals who are often non-compliant with the edicts they've established hence deserving of their fates which will be ghastly and abysmal if you listen you can hear their dismal cries upon the wind

on a sofa foul and blotted built by crones on blasted heaths there sits a monkey who's been trained to be a stand-in for the host who'll raise a toast in praise of hordes of broken spirits who now hover in the ether dumb and speechless and the hostess who'd been forced to run away and then discover she'd been banished to eternal putrefaction underground where one can find her rotting coffin stuffed with dogma and a ton of kitty litter which is never ever changed and which are choking helpless tenants with their vile hateful doctrines and their stench of piss and feces which her vile inamorato thinks is fine as does his mistress both of whom have never loved just like their mothers who before them and before the throne of god who had once scorned them but whose crimes are long forgotten hence forgiven whom they once took care to worship during long abandoned rites which were obscene and went unheard by cloth-eared children who have now been forced to live beneath the streets in grimy bunkers where the nazis drew their sketches and then took their final breaths and who now double as the playthings of the harpies who once bore them all in clinics run by mobsters who'd then bilk those moms' insurance and implant these fiendish demons into wombs which were all teeming with the shards of broken glass and which would nurture all those insects who would come one day to gnaw upon the guts of clueless victims who'd been chosen not by fate but far more likely by some fishwife from wisconsin whom it's right to do our best to never name

are we all unwitting monsters? or just those who would impose the very worst upon a world which almost surely would be better off without them? those whose books are always written by and sold to white-trash morons with no insides and whose outsides are just filth composed in mud-baths drawn and quartered in a fraction of a second which is close enough for jazz which doesn't swing on sets of playgrounds full of dust and strewn with ashes they've encased in shabby urns which help to keep their horrid mouths shut in regards to all the games of life in closets which are closest to secreting all the clay which is then made into the creatures who will deign to do their bidding on a game show which was fixed but now lies broken flat as pancakes drenched in war-paint by old widows chefs and vipers spitting venom that infects them with desires which will drive them to the brink of utter madness while they're grasping at their freedom from the masters they acclaim with endless praise that is most fulsome at the same time they are busy rubbing fat and bloated bellies filled with gruel which has grown rancid and about which they are mocked and scorned by all those selfsame masters who stand frightful in their guilt and from whom one ought run away because within them there's no good but only bitterness and seeking after truths they know are lies which were invented long ago by apparitions who had once displayed charisma but are now just propaganda for agendas of the two-bit porcine priestess who is hobbling down the stairs now that her surgery is finished which has left her somewhat hampered it is true but still quite able to spew garbage into landfills she has tended over years spent planning crimes which now have come to the fruition she intended that her spouse might comprehend that there's no way in which his nightmare can be ended or his bleeding guts e'er mended which does not require dying or at least his being beaten down by clubs in which he'll never be accepted or a member and who will then be drawn and quartered and propelled onto a scaffold where he's washed and dried and hung and will become most well and truly a dessert for birds to gorge on like medusas who can't speak nor can they sing but only shriek the music dramas of that villain richard wagner on a stage made out of newly chopped-down woodlands set aflame and then aside for it won't matter 'cause his wishes count for nothing and in fact the harpy's plan is to insure he'll be embalmed while still alive upon a bier that's made of human flesh and bone that's in a room which will be brimming full to bursting with an ancient motherlode of hungry spirits quite unyielding who will brook no independence through the days and nights of longing he will spend upon a bed of rusty nails screws and hooks on which once hung beloved paintings on the walls of former dwellings when his self was still intact before the storms which are not stressed in history books contrived by victors who enable ethnic cleansing and engage in widespread slaughter sans regret for all to see

and when those hips have healed there will be dancing in her mind and in the streets as he's unmanned in ghastly rites to be observed by vile daughters who are clones of other daughters who themselves were also daughters of the monsters who had set this thing in motion in the first place with the last laugh at the dawn of time remembered then forgotten there's no difference to be split amongst the soldiers 'neath the branches of that weeping withered barely upright tree in which poor jesus hangs suspended can you hear him? he is moaning in a wind which takes no heed but wouldn't care had it the ears to hear his cries before he dies but even he who's now abandoned (god has flown) is just a bastard who's unworthy of one's pity at the end of those three days spent on the hill where scumbag losers such as he are all impaled

so turn the page and drink a toast and dance the night away and please forget the things you've read here for the world is full of torments which reside on heads of pins which burst balloons as well as dreams that they and he had once upon a time believed might come to pass but that was then and this is now and they've awoken to a nightmare in which clouds and skies and dreams and gods are silent and their heartbeats are unsteady and their throats are all encrusted with the words they cannot utter that might matter to some soul who chanced to hear them in the dark primeval woodland where they've lived it seems forever were they able just to speak much less to beg for their salvation from their fate in that decrepit ancient forest where they'll close their eyes forever and perhaps will not be jeered at nonetheless they'll ne'er be noticed or be mourned

Sister of Mercy

On a washed up shore
Of a blasted beach,
I sing a song of me.
Ne'er heard by man,
I hope 'twill touch
The heart of my sister,
The sea.

The tide draws nearer
Ev'ry day -
To her I do commend
My hymn, most urgent,
As I pray
She will my troubles
End.

My fate's to wait
Until the hour
She sings her sweet reply -
The hour in which
She deigns to help me,
Painlessly,
To die.

Somewhere

Somewhere
There's a place setting for us -
In a celestial chorus,
Mouthing stale words
Of moldy motets,
And antibiotic-laced chicken wings -
At a soup kitchen
Down the street
From the heavenly banquet,
To the left of Chomsky,
To the right of Christ,
Where the little children suffer
On succotash,
Choked down unwillingly,
Who are then washed up zealously
In porcelain bathtubs
Made by midget veterans
In Chinese sweatshops
In back alleys
Of polluted shantytowns,
Where lead-poisoned infants awaken
Speaking creole,
Chasing butterflies,
And hunting walruses
Ripped from mangled uteruses
In botched cesareans
By demented vegan gynecologists -
Stumbling through Hell's Kitchen,
Playing invisible contrabasses,
Whistling the Meistersinger Overture,
Sipping mixed drinks,
(All the while undergoing identity, midlife, and other crises
common to mixed state disorders)
Filling their thoughts
And lining their trousers
With counterfeit coupons

From dollar stores
Owned by sullen whores
Driving stolen vehicles
Through unmanned tollbooths.

You shall know them by their good works!
(their lofty ambitions, and ill-fitting dickies)

Whisper not to me of nautical mysteries -
Rather - sing full-bodied, red-blooded arias
Written by Jew-hating pilots
Flying obsolete helicopters
Through charcoal black clouds
Stuffed to bursting
With the rancid souls
Of long-abandoned foster children
Dreaming of plush car-seats,
Succulent nipples,
And songs of vampire sirens
Dashing ancient Greek ships
On classic rocks,
Hoisted and hosted
By Ryan Seacrest,
During his salad days
Of virgin air-raids,
In which pockmarked buttocks
Are oiled by psychotic masseuses
In rented rickshaws.

Listen…

Madam Curie's furious ghost
Is playing Fauré
On the attic pump organ!
Abandoned there
Long ago
By Father,
Or Stepfather -
I can no longer recall -

Can you?
(Who actually gives a shit, anyway?)

The days of black roses on the Rhine -
Daughters whose cheeks
Have been freshly drained
By lascivious pink maidens
In bras of meticulously arranged seaweed
Bought at markets
Dripping
Fulsome and wet
With the saliva
Of raccoon dogs,
Who now hang winsomely
From meticulously arranged meathooks
Bought and paid for
By diffident young women
Whose parents' first instinct
Was to drown them
In polluted rivers
In dead of night -
Hungry as they were for sons
Who would nurse them
Through their last days
Of confusion and misery.

Weialala, weialala
Weialala, weialala
Heia leia wallala la!

Life goes on...

Weia la wallala walla la la how the life goes on...

Sonnet ("I stare into the Night's abyss...")

I stare into the Night's abyss - the Night's abyss stares back -
Compelled to walk these dreary streets, alone -
When suddenly I hear a pinging text come from my phone -
Someone that I care about, cares back.
For many years, I've felt I was defeated, washed-up, done,
That all that once was sweet is now a chore -
That nothing's left but games of chess with Death upon the shore,
That never into someone I might run
Who might, by her example and her words, help me attend
To that to which too long I had been blind -
That if I'm kind to someone, that they might, to me, be kind -
That I can have, and be, a loving friend.
Perhaps some flecks of light in me have managed to survive -
The nighttime sky seems suddenly alive.

The abysmal epiphany - long ignored, and long overdue

My birth I never could recall,
Though later I learned how
I emerged from out this spinning rock,
With sweat upon my brow.

I bellowed, wailed, wept hot tears,
And clamored to be held -
But no one heard, or seemed to care,
When these things were withheld.

I jumped the railings of my cell,
And soon began to crawl
My way upon the hardwood floor
Of a long and joyless hall

Where gradually I gained the strength
To manage standing straight
Enough, to beg for stale morsels
Dumped upon a plate.

I left that place, a ghostly shade,
Wounded, and depressed,
Persevering on my own,
And, hoping for the best

I knocked upon a stranger's door
To slake my painful thirst -
He evil eyed me warily,
Spat at me. and cursed.

At a farmhouse further down the road,
I sought a crumb of bread -
But the farmer quickly slammed the door
And chased me out, unfed.

I knocked upon a schoolhouse door,
Begging, nay demanding
Some reason for this state of things,
Beyond his understanding.

But the fact was he was bound in chains,
This paragon of learning -
Chains which everyone but he
Had no hardship discerning.

Further on, I spied a church,
And knocked upon its gate -
But when the priest appeared, he too
Was stooped beneath a weight

Which crushed his thirst for inquiry,
And left him quite unable
To do much more than offer me
A wafer at his table

In which he never had believed,
For which he had no passion -
Though he it was that offered something
Small out of compassion.

Others plunged out of the sky,
Shocked by what they saw -
Struggling not to fall into
The monstrous gaping maw

Which makes of all men's fondest dreams
Carrion and dust,
And stops their mouths with grime and filth,
With horror and disgust.

And so I walked back through the night
To that first stranger's door -
To where my journey had begun
So many years before.

I cast my gaze up to the sky,
And asked the Lord above
For sustenance, or hope of rest,
For mercy, or for love.

The blood-red sky was mute and grim -
The ground began to swell -
Then opened up a steaming pit,
Through which I slid to Hell.

I knocked three times on Satan's door,
And asked what was my sin
To merit being flayed alive -
Eliciting a grin

Which became a shriek of ecstasy,
Of ridicule, and scorn,
Of loathing, and of mockery
For all who had been born.

"Blame your self-indulgent parents,
Who never gave a thought
To all the wretchedness with which
All human life is fraught -

Who mindlessly perpetuated
Earth's most ancient crime,
Who yanked a peaceful spirit into
This farce as old as time -

And blame yourself no less, you fool,
'Tis far too late to mourn
Your hovering o'er their filthy bed,
And craving to be born.

This is the fate of Everyman,
Who lusts and yearns for breath -
A vile, filthy Purgatory,
Atoned for with his Death."

The Butterfly and the Walrus
(A brief excerpt from the "Annals of Insomniac Cerebral Flatulence" - Fall, 2012)

Henry, it's long past time to leave the woods. Cease your silly prattlings and pointless jottings. Mommy has cooked your favorite supper of warm lentil gruel.

And, by the way, a Butterfly is no more spiritual than a Walrus. Absolute folly, Henry! A Butterfly has a brain the size of a pin, upon which no angels deign to dance. They are but natures over-coiffed, Parisian harlots, impaled for all eternity in one of Nabokov's scrapbooks, like patients etherized upon tables.

And no one knows better than you, Henry, that the Walrus, that undisputed master of frozen Tantric yoga, constantly copulates, ferociously, with his harem of bemused females, to whom he reminisces about his days with the Carpenter. That bloody bastard, needless to say, was batshit bonkers, always cross, and constantly picking at his nails, the scourge of the neighborhood. He knew full well, and was more than a little embarrassed about it, that, were it not for the kindness and foresight of Mr. Rogers, hordes of the Calvary cavalry might very well have been lost.

At sea, men contract scurvy and await sirens. Wailing in the dead of night, fireman rescue still-suckling infants, cruelly abandoned in the treetops. When the wind blows, all bets are off. With her head in hand, the archer dares not aim for the apple, now fallen to the ground.

Of being we must not speak. Softly, but carrying a big stick, we confront a wasteland of refuse. To comprehend such matters, one must concentrate deeply, while there is still time. On my side, there is absence, an abscess, a void. Fifth Avenue, during rush-hour, is a sore sight for the eyes.

Have it your way. To go, to boldly go, under pressure, into the men's room of your wintry discontent, when all around you are losing theirs, is an art, and certainly no business. Like show business, it's none of your affair.

148

Of the heart, it is said that it wants what it wants. Upon a mattress, lay a wondrous girl, knitting her alabaster flesh of flaxen straw. Men are not like dogs, who never ask for whom they bark.

A lounger loiters listlessly, lazily licking his lopsided loins. Cloth is hard to come by these days, now that the Warsaw resource wars have begun, what with their tawdry bowdlerizations of the Bedouin Beguine.

Oh my - the Walrus seems to have cast a Paul upon the proceedings.

Goo goo ga joob.

Elation, love, honor, disaster relief, black humor, in sickness and in hell, till Death do we part. Our hair, on one side or the other, always manages to look funny. That you mentioned it comes as no shock. Treatment will be necessary. Evil is a apparent. Who abuses his child, abuses a universe queerer than we can imagine.

Nothing to kill or die for.

Bang, bang, shoot, shoot.

The piano player bids you farewell

You needn't.

Reciprocate.

The descent of a man

Once atop the mountain, I asked her to do a topless "fashion shoot" - play-acting of a sort which had never occurred to me with any other woman. I did not question why such a strange request gurgled, involuntarily and uneasily, out of my throat. It was a bizarre and thoroughly uncharacteristic request for me, yet one that was utterly in line with the manufactured theatrical hypocrisy that had been choking my better instincts since the beginning of this tacky soap opera - this godawful, screechy melodrama, that I seemed to have somehow signed on to - since those very first, purple, wannabe Emily Brontë letters. A melodrama in which one of the protagonists spoke with a wild, repetitive, rehearsed, and disingenuous exuberance, signifying and evoking nothing. Nothing other than a vague dread in my bowels which I had yet to understand. This nebulous terror was not (yet) of being seduced by some malevolent harpy, who hid her fangs and agendas even from herself. The worry was that I was being bewitched and narcotized by my own stupidity. The stuff of tragedy? No - of farce.

She obliged. I knew she would. It was clearly marked, in both our scripts, after all. The part of me that knew she would oblige was the very same part which knew full well that I should turn tail and bolt down the mountain like a horror-struck fawn fleeing a ravenous wolf. She was lovely. Or so most men would claim. My mind "appreciated" her beauty, yes - but only in the manner of a schoolboy who has been instructed by an overtired and underpaid high-school teacher in all the orthodox reasons one should declare the Pietà a masterpiece. Off came the blouse. And then that blouse was predictably swung around in a manner doubtless cribbed from some two-bit actress starring in some noxious rom-com. Glazed watching, with a hint of disbelief and disgust. Followed by more cringe-worthy posing. I did my best to look as if I were entranced, then looked away. I forced a disingenuous smile, then grabbed a camera with which to hide my face, which must have been dripping full of an unambiguous duplicity any normal woman would have recognized.

The lake was obscured in the distance by trees and mist. The silence was eerie, threatening - full of a wisdom it knew full well but which it took care to hide, and which manifested only in a vague, uncanny atmosphere of menace. Oh, for some sound, any sound! Of nature, of creature, of branches crashing to the ground, of wind whistling through those branches ominously or sweetly, it mattered not, of some human, any human - a backpacking pair of hippies, a buzz saw in the distance, a maniacal serial killer asking for a light - anything to mask the silence screaming in my brain that this was wrong, this was dangerous, that I must get the fuck away. And when it began to become apparent that no such diversion was to be forthcoming, I began to yearn for some mindless, lewd gnawing in my gut sufficient to overcome my hesitation and wish to flee - some bestial, overwhelming urge to fuck her. To fuck her or not to fuck her, that was clearly the question. Whether 'tis nobler to impale oneself on a harpoon, play my part in this obviously manufactured travesty, or to flee. To fuck and surely die as a result, or to cut and run, before the trap had fully closed and I was even more helpless. More lethargic, indifferent, frozen watching. And embarrassment for her - she was ridiculous. Did she not realize how ridiculous she was? I had become a rock with eyes which watched my mouth move in shock and disbelief, a mouth of which it had had no previous awareness. I watched it utter words of hollow, hypocritical praise, all the while desperately wishing to be rock, and only rock, once again. Words that anyone with a modicum of intuition would have recognized as forged and counterfeit - words inviting the catastrophe to come.

There was finally the relief of turning around, of coming down the mountain. Of hearing a buck in the distance staking out its territory with a mangled cry. Of wishing I were he. The longing, when rounding a turn and nearing a cliff, to ditch my part in this godforsaken movie.

On our way down, we arrived at what looked like a beaver pond. The air was still. My sneakers were sopping wet from the sink hole I had stepped in. Dusk, bats, squeals from creatures known and unknown - in the air, in the trees, in the pond - the sound of creaking branches in the distance. Sounds - finally! Sounds to compete with the dread-filled voices in my head. And suddenly, there he was - a beaver cutting a soundless swath through the pond, his eyes above water. Either a beaver, a gentle, swimming dog, or perhaps a stalking serpent. He slapped the water with his tail, signifying everything. Everything I knew, but couldn't yet admit to myself or act upon. There was a sensibleness in him which I searched for in vain within myself.

We are fools, interlopers, suffocating in our mindless internal chatter, which so rarely tells us the truth - we can't hear our own lives dropping to the forest floor, much less a pin. There he was, seemingly all-knowing - there IT was, the stillness at the center of everything. I was in it. The effortless rightness and profundity of the stars, the night sky, the croaking frogs. I was still beside her, but light years distant - everything that is of any worth within me had abandoned her and was now only here and in this moment. I could have died then, knowing that moment. The problem was that I would forget it, and be unable to die as a result. The voice in my head now said, nay, demanded - "Tarry..." And so we did. Alone, at last! Yet together, in her mind, which seemed to not at all register my absence. For an hour? For a lifetime? When she spoke, it became an eternity. For all the wrong reasons.

When we returned, I learned that it was as I had already been repeatedly taught to expect, and had finally grasped it was to be. And at that moment, in my mind's ear, I heard my own voice, as clearly and as brutally honest as was possible at that time, given its still-limited information - "So don't sleep next to me after we fuck, Kaley, I understand, no problem! Because outside this cabin, there's a meteor shower, and the sky is laughing - why would I possibly worry about what is to come, about who you are, about what you want, about what you are planning, about what you are planning without even realizing you are planning it. And dear God! - PLEASE stop with all those laughably ludicrous, clichéd, studied, faux-seductive looks and moves - they are absurd, preposterous! Why would I endure a round of overly serious sex, full of phony protestations, apishly over-rehearsed sighs and facial expressions, just for the sake of a dopey little orgasm? The feeblest of payoffs for what I would be forced to endure in order to arrive at it? Why? When comets are racing through empty space, and stars are exploding in the heavens? Listen, fool! To the crickets, the night's hum, its orgiastic, enveloping song, its dark, compelling invitation to forget, its delicious stupor. Our bodies could come together in what you are bound to call an "exploding supernova" not long after, some all-important, cosmos shattering event that proclaims our love for all eternity, some bit of purple nonsense you've cribbed from the cheesy hokum you imbibe constantly - all that shit you constantly say, can't possibly mean, and know is secondhand. Have you noticed, once having declared such gibberish, what happens next, almost invariably? To both of us? To absolutely everyone after they fuck??? That we have to take a piss? Perhaps stub our little toe on the way to the bathroom, and begin to obsess upon whether it's broken or not? That we're assaulted by the vile stench of sweat and spittle? Suddenly embarrassed and disgusted by our bodies, and overwhelmed by 'post-coital tristesse'? But then again, Galen said, 'Every animal is sad after coitus except the human female and the rooster.' So perhaps that is unlikely. Yet there is also Spinoza, whom you would dismiss, along with every other philosopher, because you misread a chapter or two of Wittgenstein in college and use him as an excuse whenever you don't want to deal with any challenging or troubling thoughts. Apparently, everything is mere wordplay until you're attempting to manipulate me through their use. Is this wordplay? 'After the enjoyment of sensual pleasure is passed, the greatest sadness follows.' Or Schopenhauer's maxim - 'Directly after copulation the devil's laughter is heard.' I know perfectly well what would be more than likely to happen, were we to fuck now. And why. And with a certainty far greater than ordinarily - were I to be lying next to, much less inside of, YOU. Death, desiccation, and the abyss.

All I want is to not be here, to not be anywhere at all, to not BE at all - to be lost in the ecstasy of the night, in silence and oblivion. Not the awful silence that was hysterically screaming just a few hours ago, 'Run! Get away!' The silence that will carry me home to when and where I was not - the silence which held me in its loving arms before I was born, and to which I shall return."

But of course I said none of this. The fact was that I'd already folded like a house of cards in a tornado, and was soon to be dragged to a landfill, from whence I'd be eventually carted on a donkey, whipped and brutalized by Kaley to do her bidding, down a long, agonizing road to meet his destiny - to be incinerated alive, in Hell.

The fluttering of wings in the dream-filled night

The moment you declare a passion dead
Is the moment you've indulged a lie,
A ruse you've devised to soothe yourself -
Passions sleep, but never die.

They wake you in the dead of night,
With a tingling limb, a note, a word -
The fluttering of wings, in the dream-filled night,
Of a sensuous, singing forest bird

Who slows her flight above each town
To search the beating hearts beneath her,
In hopes of saddling Pegasus
With riders worthy of the ether.

You'll recognize her plaintive song,
Her yearning cries, from dusk till dawn -
And when she comes, some windswept night,
You must react - she'll soon be gone.

For if not you, she'll seek another -
Who bolts through heavens matters not.
If she chooses to embrace you for a high-flown moment,
You must strike, once the iron's been roused and is hot.

The hateful harridan

Someone tie my daughter's tubes before it is too late -
She's on her good behavior, and has even found a mate.
Hence the sense of urgency - to act and not to wait,
In order that we spare that child a ghastly, dreadful fate.

That thing, that hateful harridan, by monstrous devil nursed,
By selfsame fiend instructed, by Nature surely cursed,
Will exercise her blackest arts, in which she's now well-versed
Upon that poor, defenseless child, to whom she'll do her worst.

The hope is that he'll end up in some other woman's bed,
Or, barring that, get so pissed off by something she has said
He cuts her brake lines, poisons her, or shoots her in the head -
Alas! It's far more likely they will procreate instead.

But what would be the implications with respect to me?
Consider all the karmic threads that would connect to me!
I have to engineer a plan for his vasectomy,
Or bribe that witch to buy into a hysterectomy
Which gouges out that sack of slime which lurks between her
legs -
Then light a fire on the beach, and toss in all her eggs.

The hazardous wager

How to even begin to tell you what it felt like to play the piano with you sitting beside me? With your warmth enveloping me from behind, yet seemingly emanating from everywhere - from above, below, inside, outside - whooshing into and through me, to fill the entire universe? I cannot possibly manage it. I will never have the words. It was the deepest validation as a person I have ever experienced, as if there would always be a place for me in this world where I belong, where I'm wanted, and where I want and need to be - a place I could not possibly ever before have imagined existing. There is a delicious, tender, and tingling cloak of your warmth that I'm wearing still, all these many hours later. I see your smile right in front of me, shimmering and luminous in the ether, and your deep, soulful, wet, and heavy-lidded brown eyes. I still hear the ecstatic music of your laughter careening through my brain, echoing, as it did last night, in duet with the punch-drunk wind, wildly whistling through the rafters. I, too, am drunk - drunk with, and lost in, the exquisite curves, seductive hills, and valleys of your sweet, creamy, luscious, and ultimately terrifying body. Who the hell are you? You're a good angel, right? Or is this a trick? Because I see that my shirt has been pulled up, I know not when, other than that it must have been when you were here, and that a bull's-eye has been etched onto my heart with red magic marker. And, from the time I first met you, I could not but mark the Amazonian crossbow which dangles constantly from your strong and sensuous shoulders, stocked, as it is, so full and well with blood-red arrows... These are hardly Cupid's arrows. Is my name on one? More than one? It must be. For how could it be otherwise? What sense would there be in any of this, were it not so? And yet I could go now, I can go now - without a care, without a single regret. I have tasted the nectar of the gods, the ambrosia of nonbeing, the delicious stupor of obliteration. Who the hell are you? Passion, peace, a taste of immortality, and of perfection? Or Death - oblivion... Either way, I'm in.

The Pale Child - a collection of 36 poems

I.

As night falls they carry my dead father from his bed
Through the quiet rustling of leaves and the gentle breeze
They whisper to one another
The death people
In the insipidly earnest twilight
His voice echoes faintly through the night air
A bell tolls
Harsh and bitter
In my aching heart
They ask if I would like to see him
(If there were a god, how unspeakable this all would be
How filled with awe and remorse and the agony of irrevocable loss
I would be)
But there is only the black night
No comets
No purple flames
Only the hum of a ravaged ambulance
Stumbling mute beneath a deaf heaven

158

II.

Tentative footsteps of a broken child
The peal of bells
The silence of despair
I have come this way before
Fearful and alone, always alone
Nights full of anguish
The empty and treacherous camaraderie of solitude
(Look - the blind mother steals through the dark wood
with the broken bones of her dead child)
My smashed mouth cannot speak
Though my scorched eyes see
In the dusky bloodshot hours
How she eats his heart
Again and again
While the mute creatures of the night dream their purple
oblivion
God weeps impotent tears
Yet sends no fiery spirit to avenge this crime
This savage feast
The body decays and with it the mind
But always the soul engulfed in dread
Its broken jaws moaning and sobbing in the dew-drenched dawn
Clutching at every last tendril of dream
Now matter how poisonous
In dread of waking

III.

I too had heard the blackbirds calling
Through icy winds on starlit nights
But that was long ago
Before they vanished
Without warning
And I ceased believing
In the midnight mutterings of birds
Their voiceless velvet lies
That once drew me on
In a more voluptuous time
On starless nights
In caves of dread
Eyes wet with tears
And the dew of mornings that never arrived
Mute creatures of night
Merciless phantoms of space and time
Have you no word for me other than oblivion
Honey-sweet like the milky tingling of freshly cut flesh
Now that the quivering ecstasy of blood and bone are no longer
mine?
I shall mourn this night
Like a newborn babe
With a cry that shall
For an instant
Light dead galaxies

IV.

The cave of childhood glows warm and distant
Through the hiss of falling leaves and trains going nowhere
Contemptuous branches conceal the tired sun
It is the moon's time
The time to burrow deep into the fecund earth for warmth
I know this place
It is my soul
An evil labyrinth of solitary rooms and half-heard music
A jumble of memory and longing
The dark honey of a faceless woman's song
My imbecilic heart wildly clutching
The musky warmth of a fragrant grave
Its cruel inviting mouth
Its mercy

V.

How you reached through time and space
To grab my soft white throat
How you dropped me
Blue and frozen
By the side of the warm shroud
In which one fair as I
Should have only slept peacefully
How you left your eyes half-open
In mists and fog
Of pain and longing
And withdrew your demon fingers
Into the cruel and sunless void
In which you wait now
For me
I listen for your voice
By the old stones
In the murmurs of forests
In the lamentations of birds
You run from me in dreams
Behind a thousand masks
The shadow of beauty
In bare branches
You taunt and soothe me
You've forgotten
It doesn't matter
Calm and quiet
You sit impassive
By my bed
Mix my hot tears
With the blood
That stops your throat
Kiss my weary brow
With your ice-blue lips
Tell me
Sing to me

Where has the time all gone to
I will dream this black and lonely room
For a moment longer
Until we sing together
By the cool clear mountain river
The taste of oblivion on our tongues
Our souls
Fused and incandescent
In the setting sun

VI.

When night comes
Good and evil clutch at one another
In a wild and voluptuous embrace
(The echoing shriek of owls)
Linger, merciful twilight
Pain and death are children of the sun
Whose fiery demons pierce flesh
But do not singe its source
Through the scrim of dream
God dispenses what mercy he can
Mute
Ravaged
Terrified
An impotent spectator
Of His own absurd creation
A fiction
An hourglass
The flesh of a saint
The skull of a child
Ancient footsteps
Unheard since the world began
Eternal lamentation
The sobbing of ashes
My soul

164

VII.

The soul is a stranger in this dark city
The wind blows cruelly
In black sleep
The waters mutter ancient lies
Of distant angels
This is an evil and bitter place
Full of signs and omens
The streets crooked with regret
You travel alone
With the eyes of scavengers upon you
The watchman snug in his blood-drenched bed
(Angels have no souls
hence are content)
Walk quickly now
From hearth to hearth
Fill your belly
With shards of glass
Shared with dark creatures
Over cold fires
The steeple bells are ringing
The sky is alive
Look -
The stars have come
With their shimmering promise
To release your suffocated self
From its damp dungeon
Into the cool and fragrant breeze
Of oblivion

VIII.

You rise from the dead
Night after night
Only to ignore me
You comprehend everything
And nothing
You are a half-swallowed
Poorly digested
Particle
Of cruelly unsatisfying sustenance
Yet
In the end
I shall be your supper

IX.

In the evening
The orphans climb the ancient mountain
Entombed in private nightmares
The keening of dead mothers
The cackling of nightbirds
Swirl like ravenous fire
Through the night sky
The twilight is magnificent
Menacing
Meaningless
Listen -
Beneath the cold and unmerciful ground
The blindworms are shrieking
The earth is whirling
Sobbing
Bleeding
The infinite echo of the dead
Hungry for oblivion
The night is swarming with spirits
Who cannot rest
Will never rest
This life of yours
This brief life
Which stuffs you full of pomp and distraction
Savor it
For soon
You too
Will be shrieking
Through the night air
For all eternity

X.

If death be but deepest sleep
Let the icy waves of eternity come now
Benumb me with their voluptuous tendrils
See the ravaged boatmen
How frantically they paddle
Blocked from the warmth of the sun
By indignant phantoms
How desperately they embrace
One another's luxurious lying limbs
And if those hovering shades could sing
Through their blood and dread-clogged throats
Would they not sing
Of rounded sleep
Of dusky violets
And murmuring streams?
Rather their prayers
Would rip instead the indifferent moon
From the imbecilic heavens
Splatter the earth
With purple blood
And endless lamentation
Capsize the petrified boat
With its storm-drenched hope
And infinite sorrow
Its vanity and illusions
Watch it shatter in the vengeful embrace
Of the uncaring sea
Its human refuse
Strewn upon sinister shores
Under cold and distant stars
Where the newly dead
Wait
Furious and insatiable

XI.

At twilight
The hermit emerges from his blue cave
To caress the evening breeze
With his bony hands
As the sun kisses the horizon
So too does his soul his ravaged body
Why does the earth not tremble
And the clouds not weep?
Listen -
It is autumn
Only the racing thoughts
Of a departing consciousness
The sound of crushed leaves
The lonely call of the owl
The scurrying of famished rats
Scrambling greedily
As the dark wind
Howls
For its supper

XII.

They come and go
The hot tears
In a dark and solitary room
A frozen child calls for its mother
(Good and evil gestate
in the womb of night
and are born into the yellow glare
of the morning sun)
Look for the souls
Of buried angels
When the snows begin to melt
Rising like translucent ravens
Towards the incandescent moon
Their delicious and quivering madness
With its dark and shuddering tongues
Its spasms of delight
In forgotten folds
Of the undertaker's severest garment
The spirit of the once rosy child
Strains its blinded eyes
Towards the light
Which has betrayed it
The reprieve of sleep
The ecstatic song
Of risen angels
Throbbing in the night sky
Let him die then
Impaled on the wind
Of riotous and infernal sound
In a fiery dance
Of seared flesh
And unanswered prayers
Food for wild birds
Passing over dark water

XIII. The Pale Child

How long have I been dead
Roaming through sunless catacombs
Catching sight of lonely phantoms
In cruel mirrors
Wandering unobserved
Through brazen sideshows
Of twisted flesh
The pale child lies awake
Waiting vainly for the sun
To rise
Luminous
In his beating heart
Love devoured him long ago
Made of his soul
A rotting husk
Rooting aimlessly
Amidst evil haystacks
Perhaps you've seen him
The pale child
Though you'd likely not recall him
How long have I been dead
Said the pale child
To no one in particular
His timid song
Hides behind purple mists
And the inhuman music of twilight
Listen...
The prayer of a bramble-born boy
Impaled on a thornbush
For all eternity

XIV.

Something long forgotten
Has roused itself
From its musty coffin
In the rotting house
Which mutters half-heard answers
To unasked questions
Once more the sobs and pleas
The sweet suffocation
The fitful sleep
In the frozen lake
A delicious woman
With the moist and musky scent of evil
Heavy upon her
Sits drumming her fingers
In the dark café of dream
Oh how your ravaged soul shivers and glistens
As it casts off its grief-stricken body

XV.

A time will come
When there will be no lamentations
Over warm corpses
No anguished cries
Of the freshly bereft
To disturb our sleep
The quivering dance
Of life and death
Will be as nothing
Oh the cold metallic sweetness of galaxies
The luminous orbits of eyeless comets
The radiant smiles of dead children

XVI.

There's blood on the wind
The wolves smell it
Falcons carry off abandoned children
Who cry
As the primeval fireball once cried
Whipped into an unwanted existence
By an unrepentant demon
The earth is evil
It is molten
Hungry
Vengeful
Dripping a pestilence
Which smashes hope
And crushes desire
They scurry to frozen caves
The survivors
Lashed from behind
By troubled dreams
Of rats gnawing bone and star
Now that he has cast them off
God's savage laughter
Echos
Infinite cruel and cold
Through the lonely vacuum
Of an abandoned universe

XVII.

The lovers cross the enchanted lake
In a plain black boat
A cloaked figure at the helm
The fetid wind in his face
The cries of crickets in his ears
His charges oblivious
Of the gruesome sunset
Impatient
To devour them
The waters murmur
Exhausted and solemn
From the abandoned island
The animals watch
Sullen and impassive
They explode
Like drunken supernovas
Reeling through space
For an ecstatic moment
And then it is done
The boat translucent as glass
The water cold and full of filth
Yet reflecting perfectly
The image of two cadavers in the pale moonlight
Who believed
The paltry soul
Was something other
Than a ragged outcast
To be flung
Without mercy
In tatters on a dark shore

XVIII.

The tired horde of toothless women
Tramps darkly over the crumbling cobblestone path
Their eyes folded in fetid labyrinths of withered flesh
Their shoes tattered and damp with the blood of twenty
centuries
(Night falls
The rain hisses angrily)
Yet in their breasts beat hearts
Which remember a time
When men had souls
When nightingales sang songs
Of indescribable beauty
In tones of rapturous stillness
Their minds are a jumble of pain and longing
Yet their ravaged ears hear nothing
Though the sound of rain and blood
On mute unfeeling stone
Is deafening
And the songbird's ecstatic lamentation
Is drowned in the din of the distant slaughterhouse

XIX.

The freshly strewn snow
Covers the bloody footprints
Of the terrified women
Who beat their breasts
And beseech the moon
Their child has vanished
Borne on the backs of ecstatic stallions
Swallowed in the velvet stillness
Far from the covetous curses of the living
Their unending lamentations
And the dark deceit
Of their ugly lust
Like all saints
From time immemorial
He too kissed the lid
Of the voluptuous eye
Which beckoned and consumed him
As it slyly
And irrevocably
Winked itself
Out of existence

XX.

A careless moonlit stroll
The sudden familiar terror
Refracted through blighted senses
The smell of cheap perfume
And stale cigarette smoke
The jeering laughter
Of soulless flesh
The slovenly applied lipstick
Running in rivers
Like the molten lava
At the earth's core
Like blood
Pumped from evil's stale womb
Through the world's beating heart
To the infernal whorehouse
Bought
Paid for
And abandoned
The cackling of zombies
The ravaged vault of heaven
The prison of dream

XXI.

The old ones
Grow silent
Die
The orphan
Like a wraith at sunset
Stuffs his pockets with warm bread
His melancholy prayers
To god the father
(Twice-orphaned he)
Echo through the mists of time
A lonely strand
In earth's cruel symphony
Birds drop soundlessly from the night sky
On the abandoned corpses
Like a healing and redeeming rain

XXII.

It is wonderful
To stagger
Posthumous and drunk
Over graves
Faintly lit
By sad stars
And mournful moons
The living are lonely and unreal
Broken puppets
Wandering phantoms
Who clutch and grimace
Toil and spawn
Wither and die
Spirits of the unborn
Intone their jealous lamentations
Upon the night air
Into the loins and minds
Of the living
(The mindless chirping of insects
The imbecilic sighs of lovers)
All the while the soul
Purged of desire
By the knowledge of death
And the flame of solitude
Floats free and boundless
In an ethereal cadenza
Of silence

XXIII.

In the evening
The dead descend
From the abandoned shore
Into the delicious waters
Of the black lake
Sighing and grateful
As jealous angels
Look down from above
Seeking innocence to violate
With their spiny wings
And rough embraces
At the candlelit altar
Of the spectral church
A blind child prays
For the soul
Of her newly dead mother
Galaxies hum ecstatic dirges
Older than time
An impotent god strains to catch their echo
In the cruel and frozen vacuum
Of endless space

XXIV.

On damp pillows
In shuttered rooms
The delicate limbs of lovers
Entwine themselves
Like the dark branches
Of twisted trees
Like musty cobwebs
Long abandoned
By petrified spiders
In half-lit mirrors
Hooded figures wander
In a sunless world
Frozen and separate
The dead man and his wife
Arrange the rotting furniture
To resemble the shimmering room
In which they first met
And always the self
Suffocating and black
Fastened to the soul
Like a mourner's waistcoat
When once I took your slender and pale hands
Those many years ago
The blue fire in your half-lidded eyes
Illumined only what I chose to see
Evil gestates
Silently and purposefully
In the black womb of night
Desperate bones
Tattered and leprous
Struggle to climb
From crumbling family vaults
To breathe again
The lies
And musky scent
Of youth

XXV.

At that time
The night bristled with angels
Flying through the brambles of the dark forest
Whipping the furious wind with their filthy wings
And cursing the one who made them
But now the night is an empty and soulless thing
The clockwork hunt of owls
The unkind silhouettes of wounded trees
The pallid faces of lost loved ones
The peace of imbeciles
The silence is devastating and immense
The children have all fled
To blue caves and deserted steppes
The apparitions who once embraced them
Only to drop them from black clouds onto stony paths
(All the while murmuring of their selfless love)
Have disappeared or died
They tremble in their loneliness
Thrash about in fitful sleep
Yearn to have the dead touch them one last time
Before they recede
Soundlessly and irrevocably
Into the vanishing rooms of dream
Did the black sun once warm them?
In the moonlit mirror
Their hair is stiffened with mud and tears
Their eyes hollow with the hunger of longing

XXVI.

On a ravaged trail
In a stony mountain pass
The newly resurrected meet
They clutch desperately at one another
Their milk-white flesh
Shimmering in the blood-red sun
At the foot of the orphan's pale green bed
The cadaverous crone
Waits
Cruel and impassive
Ravenous and frozen
There are cries heard and uttered in sleep that echo through
galaxies
The lamentations of unwilling bones
Emerging from abandoned graveyards
The lullabies of malignant mothers
Sung
Tender and cancerous
To helpless infants

XXVII.

The cry of the abandoned cat
Blasts fitful sleep
It is nothing
It is your doom
The corrosive murmur of angels
Mute and cruel
Flightless and lost
Like your soul
Your body
With its throat full of silt
And its ears stopped with earth
The cruel counterpoint of unheard voices
Choked with longing
Calling from dead stars
Across vast spaces
We are all apparitions in the dark and silent night
Deaf
Singing
And consumed with loneliness
The road home is shrouded
In mists of wishing
The terrifying peal of bells
The moans of the heavenly choir
The world is an appalling mistake

XXVIII.

The lonely child
Stirs the lifeless waters
Of the deserted pond
A single white lily
At its center
Too weak to wade
Through its blasted sludge and silt
His misshapen reflection
Chastises him green and fetid
The waters are quiet again
In the dark forest
The lament of a nightbird seeking its mate
The tears of a ravaged earth

XXIX.

She murmurs to me
From a half-lit world
The life seeping from her body
Her soul would wrench itself free
Hover in cloistered crevices
Of vaulted cathedral ceilings
(Wounds which pierce the heart
do not touch the spirit)
Her lips are wet and inviting
Her eyes fast closing
In ecstatic stillness
The rapture of saints
The torrents of blood
Mindless ravenous purple blood
Gushing through the smug streets
Of the deserted city
She has become
The most delicate and fragrant of songs
Intoned by phantoms
Who ride free
On the icy winds
Of stars
Lean your silvery forehead down
To kiss my ravaged brow
Whisper your ecstatic gravesong
In my famished ear
This one last time
Take me
Ravish me
Smother me
O my love

XXX.

Deepest night
Angels sing dark songs of ecstasy
Leaves shiver restlessly
Quickened by the silvery wind
You stand before me
With your tear-drenched eyes and blood-red lips
As you have stood before me always
Before the moon ripped itself free from the belly of the earth
To glisten through your shimmering and luminous spirit
We had become one another
Wolves coupling
Savage and eternal
Our red blood mingling and streaming towards heaven
We who were never born can never die
God is here with us
Singing
The earth is still
Listening
Trembling
The pitiless offertory of unending anguish and rapture
O sweet and milky madness
Let it end now
Here
Like this
In the tender half-lidded blue twilight
Of oblivion

XXXI.

My sister's shadow steals like mist through the somber forest
Her grief suspended like icicles on severed branches
Her dark laments echoing
Through musty bedrooms in distant cities
Where couples devour one another
Distraught and oblivious
Of the unborn
Who surround them
Their voices pleading on the dark wind of disdainful night
Their breath pounding in the frantic pulse of feverish loins
Sister
I too have fled into the thorny wilderness
Pursued by red wolves and evil falcons
Seeking black ecstasy
Dewdrops of blood
Sleep
And death

XXXII.

The gurglings of the dying man
Seep into the night air
From beneath the black and indifferent water
In its distorted reflection
Of the star-filled heavens
Hungry angels gather
To hold the world
In a crystal bowl
Of cruelty and madness
To fling the exhausted sleeper
Into the savage storm
Of swarming souls
In the town the sobs of the terrified woman
As she searches for her stolen child
In the forest the shrieks of the furious falcon
As he devours his frail prey
How ridiculous the gesticulations of mannequins
Wrapped in winding sheets
And impaled on church turrets
The cosseted child
The sacrificial lamb
How malignant the mind of God
How sordid the spectacle of His creation

XXXIII.

In the abandoned room of childhood
Under an evil canopy of blue stars
The chatter of demons
Wafts through the lilac breeze
Through the ancient glass and decrepit walls
The terror and silence
The glazed and hooded eyes
Of mute faces
Buried in musty books
The emaciated retchings
Of the cadaverous mother
No one had ever been kind to him
Full to bursting
With hate lust and dread
The wish to violate every reflection and creature
The bellyache of the soul's eternal hunger
The perpetual prayer for peace
Had the wraith not whispered her wish to him
Hissed it in his famished ear
With her wet lips and purple tongue
Again and again?
The venomous hiss
Of intimacy
The boundless betrayal
Of love
The weight of stones
Lashed to infants
Thrown in black ponds
By sinister widows
The last ripple of him who should never have been
Swallowed in the shadow of a sick moon
On still water

XXXIV.

His mother's dark figure blackens the doorway
Spiteful and unyielding
Grieving women with distant voices and waxen faces
Bear him through warm forests
With measured steps
In the smothered sanctuary of dream
Swarms of savage men pursue him
Through crippling labyrinths
Of filth and fear
Deep within the earth
(In heaven's sepulchral sideshow)
The ravaged flesh of whores is spun
In viscous webs of violent deceit
Thrust cursed and unwilling from the rancid womb
Into the blinding glare of anguish and lust
The frigid tomb of childhood
Engulfed in the mirror's unholy flame
Legless feverish and damned
His phantom sobs and pleads with God
To let him die

XXXV.

Death enters the house with measured steps
Bearing the spurious solace
Of oblivion
He finds the radiant child
Bleeding and defenseless
By the bed
Scheming of evil
The spindly keeper beats her stone heart
Her night-shriek stolen from leprous vampires
Sleep is dark and sweet
Littered with succulent temptations and unnerving dread
Poisoned with promises and a mother's misshapen face
Death is enticing and voluptuous
A promise sung by a deceitful moon
To imbeciles
Drunk with the scent and taste
Of chastity and sorrow
Alleluia...
We are damned
All of us
With our gushing blood and blasted hearts
Numb with the pealing of bells
Struck by savage angels in dark clouds
We strut and scurry
Prattle and pray
While famished sirens with ravaged eyes
Gnash their poisoned maws
In the cruelly whistling wind
Await their appalling banquet
The guiltless
The helpless
The damned

XXXVI.

In the quiet house
The dead mother
Serves bleeding bread
To ungrateful corpses
From across the rotting table
The dazed sister
Stares
Mute with disbelief
In this house mouths have long been sewn shut
Tongues severed and served on shattered plates
Half-swallowed shards of musk-scented mirrors
Stuck in blistered throats
Bemoaning their birth
Into the blinding glare
Of a frozen sun
Oh to never have been
To sink like a stone
In a boundless sea
Of blackest night
To cast off the ravaged self
The ruthless and unreal others
To finally
Irrevocably
And forever
Forget

The Radiant Buddhist Nun –
A Diary of Idealism and Disillusionment

The Radiant Buddhist Nun - August 30, 2012

The Radiant Buddhist Nun is a human being (at least I'm fairly certain she is), who has doubtless suffered a difficult childhood, various frightening, life-threatening illnesses, and the loss of two husbands. Perhaps these things are what led her to the practice in the first place. Perhaps not perhaps, as in - it's very likely that this is so. But that is irrelevant. I've watched her meditate, and it is a fascinating experience. There is something unearthly, deeply mysterious, and extremely inspiring going on. I have terrible trouble sitting still. For one thing, and it's a pretty fatal thing: I find myself frequently thinking back to the psychological problems I encountered and induced through my having meditated as a young man. When she is meditating, she seems to be working terribly hard, yet is often smiling, as if she is bathed in some beatific light and truth. At other times, one observes what looks like an intense, soulful yearning, as she concentrates on "healing, light, compassion, death, etc." (this according to her). At no time, or so it seems to me, does she appear to be flirting with anything that might ultimately prove dangerous. Her meditation seems about as far from what I used to do, i.e., what the characteristically drooling, mantra-bleating Transcendental Meditation practitioner does, as nectar is from a 7-Eleven Slurpee. Her conception of the afterlife and personal reincarnation seem to me, at least for now, beautiful, psychologically useful, and, who am I to say - not necessarily fictions. When she speaks of a cancer-stricken child, whom she believes is experiencing karma from a previous life, it is not the moral abomination such statements almost always are, coming from the mouths of the types of folks who usually say such things. It is a deeply compassionate recognition of pain in a sentient, suffering being, who deserves our deepest kindness and humaneness now, and who did, as well, in their former, according-to-her, misguided incarnation. She has tricks of this sort, along with real insights to share, but they are quite besides the point. She, herself, is the lesson - the light, the reason to believe, to take any of this even remotely seriously. It is as if she is some sort of benevolent eagle, i.e., some higher being inhaling the filth and pollution of the world, and exhaling light, wisdom, love, and mercy. I've had one or two smart therapists over the years, but they seem just more or less talented mud-wrestlers in comparison - flailing about, trying to explain away what cannot be explained away with thoughts, words, theories, and projections, i.e., coughing up received wisdom and little else. It's far too late for me to become an accomplished meditator, in any way that would make a difference, at any rate. Not that I have any wish to be one! In fact, the thought of attempting to do so terrifies me. It's just as unlikely as my now becoming an accomplished cellist at this late stage, in any way that could or would make a difference. But one can meditate through, and in, life, as well, and this I fully intend to do. Effort brings freedom.

The Radiant Buddhist Nun - September 13, 2012

The Radiant Buddhist Nun spoke again last night. She talked of "becoming wood" - of loving, but without ever attaching. About how anger is like the flu, how one must isolate oneself from others until it passes. When I asked her whether anger was sometimes a result of hurt (admittedly a dopey, Psychology Today-level sort of question), she dismissed me out of hand - saying simply, yet firmly, that Buddhism doesn't concern itself with such matters. She told us a tale of her driving from the Berkshires to New York City, all the while chanting, "I wish to become a Bodhisattva in this lifetime". She described animals as former humans, who were now trapped in an unfortunate "lower" rebirth as a result of negative karma, and how they deserve our deepest compassion because of this. How you can see the previously human soul, if you look hard and empathically enough, in the eyes of a dog, cow, etc. I resisted the temptation to ask her how this compassion might play out when looking into the eyes of a tarantula or Komodo dragon, though it was challenging to refrain. When I asked her if she were vegan, she offered an indescribably charming giggle in response. When I asked her how an animal accumulates sufficient good karma to be reborn as a human being, the most propitious of rebirths, according to her (although I might beg to differ, if pressed), she offered only a second, indescribably charming giggle in response. When I told her of my experience, as a young man, of meeting TM teachers and practitioners, who struck me as nothing other than escape artists, with all their fatuous chatter, and that awful, vacuous deadness in their eyes - apparent zombies who spoke of aspiring to be "dead while alive", and of how horrified I was by all this - of how I had practiced TM for close to four years, stopped "cold turkey", as they say, as a result of the nagging epiphany that I, too, was becoming one of "them" - and how I, immediately after stopping, had had a very close to fatal nervous breakdown, which I attributed then, and continue to attribute now, to having become addicted to a dangerous, spiritually-deadening practice, sold by spiritual grifters and swindlers, who were offering spiritual snake oil to the world - and that this was why I had stayed away from any and all things to do with any sort of "meditation" - out of a healthy cynicism and fear, borne of experience - when I told her all these things, which have haunted me for close to forty years, she had only asinine and mindless platitudes to offer me as a response.

I went to sleep heartsick. I awoke with her loving, lovable, and compassionate presence vivid in my mind's eye. Yet today, her "lightness of being" strikes me as potentially becoming "unbearable" - that of a butterfly which is pretty, which is mindless, and which is pretty mindless - spiritual, yes, in some sense, and without question, but irresponsible and disturbingly lightweight in another - that "lightness of being" perhaps simply an "absence of thought", of depth, of "being in the world in which we all live" - a cheap and lazy escape from the filthy, sweaty, confusing, suffering planet that I, she, and all of us inhabit. An ultimately dishonest and cowardly escape. I've been watching her meditate again, watching intensely. She works very, very hard while meditating, and with great fervor. She doesn't even remotely zone out like the TM zombies of whom I was complaining earlier, and of whom I was one. This constitutes much of what has fascinated and inspired me for some weeks now. What on earth is she doing? What on earth is she working for, what is she trying to achieve? And yet this morning, I am unsure whether what she is working for is not as ultimately empty-headed, inane, and craven as those despicable TM teachers, whom I had the ill-luck of having met and taken seriously long ago - this in spite of that delightful, seductive twinkle in her eye, the exquisite music of her laughter, and her gentle, soothing voice and manner. I just don't know. I will refrain, for now, from any conclusions, and return next week. But today I am somewhat disconsolate, and, truth to tell, feeling rather silly, as if I may have remained the very same, perpetual sucker, after all these years.

Orson Welles' monologue in "The Third Man", the one in which he contrasts the respective aesthetic achievements of the Italian Renaissance with those of the isolated and peaceful nation of Switzerland keeps coming to mind. What are my values? What really matters to me? Yes, I've had a painful life. But can that justify the cowardly wish to retreat into some quasi-narcotized state of emotionally dead detachment, which snuffs out the potential for an infinitely more meaningful engagement and struggle with the world as it actually is?

Perhaps she's nothing more than a spiritual cuckoo clock after all, as Orson put it so wisely and pithily.

The Radiant Buddhist Nun - September 30, 2012

The Radiant Buddhist Nun has regained and surpassed her former radiance. Last night, she sang a perfectly imbecilic tune, with words which were almost certainly embarrassingly poor translations of, who knows, what is perhaps sublime Sanskrit poetry, when in their original form, with a simple, artless voice that cut me in half - a voice of such purity and angelic innocence that I thought the heavens would explode. When she sang Ti leading to the octave, several phrases after having repeatedly sung bTi leading to the octave, I felt as if I had left my body, and was floating over the room. And this happened over and over. She spoke, at length, about the most patent nonsense - the "Ages of Man" before written history, in which countless Buddhas had appeared, Buddhas who are presently accessible, in what I am assuming she is implying are our own depraved and fallen times, only in the meditations of the most supreme Masters, and in the topographies of various Bardos, of how the soul is "utterly distinct" from the body, etc. - a stereotypically ludicrous collection of Bronze Age and New Age jibber-jabber, which no minimally educated person would ever consider as anything other than moral allegory, which has been dumbed down, probably countless times, for the unwashed rabble, who, because they are untutored morons living in culturally bankrupt times, take it all quite literally. I had heard one of her compatriots from the Dharma center spout the same lunacy two months prior, i.e., offering nonsense of this sort as the literal truth. At that time, it was very hard not to stop my incessant, uncharitable internal chatter. Last night, my internal chatter was quite different. There was, in fact, precious little of it. Why? Because I believed and felt that I was in the presence of some sort of Saint, some sort of Saint of Consciousness, whose temporal lobe was perhaps not the brightest bulb in the neighborhood, but whose essence was indescribably divine.

The Radiant Buddhist Nun, somewhat less "Radiant" now - October 18, 2012

The Radiant Buddhist Nun is almost certainly some sort of holy person. Of this I have no doubt. She has easy and reliable access to all sorts of wonderful interior states of consciousness. And yet, she repeatedly advocates cherishing others over cherishing oneself to increase one's PERSONAL happiness, to create good karma for one's SELF, and to positively influence one's PERSONAL, future rebirths. She suggests that we, as meditators, meditate on, e.g., deformed Iraqi babies to increase our PERSONAL feelings of compassion, our PERSONAL awareness of suffering in the world. She is, shockingly, utterly unaware of the fatal contradiction and irony in all of this. She describes the ecstatic interior visions she has come to experience in her own PERSONAL mind, which, in contradistinction to her earlier stated claims, is apparently what she cherishes most. For herein lies the REAL GOAL. I had hoped and thought, up until this point, that it would have been quite the opposite, but, in the end, all of this boils down to, for the most part, "MY, MY, MY" and "ME, ME, ME". The manipulation and production of an excess of narcotizing brain chemicals - "Chicken Soup for the Selfish, Self-involved Soul".

Two stitches that a decidedly unenlightened, in her view, Médecins Sans Frontières physician places in a child's head to sew up a wound are worth more than all her, and all of her peers', narcissistic naval gazing. "Wisdom" of this sort is dispensed and valued only in overfed, First World countries. Usually on Oprah, i.e., it is, for the most part, the goal of overly self-absorbed, solipsistic, superficial "consumers".

I'm being way too harsh - of this I am certain. We all use whatever means we can grasp, believe, and hold on to to negotiate our way through this vale of tears, me very much included. But what can I do? These are the values and priorities that are ultimately jumping out of the tapestry of what she says and advocates, more and more. I will never be able to respect or even tolerate such things, least of all in myself, were I to go down such a road. I shall not return. And yet - I won't forget her, either.

The Spinster and the Mark

"Will you walk into my parlour?" said the Spinster to the Mark,
While planning, all the while, to keep her victim in the dark;
"I promise that I'll love you till the very end of time!"
Said she, while taking care to hide the nature of her crime;
"Oh no, no!" said the little Mark, well knowing 'twas a ruse,
But fantasies of rescue made it tricky to refuse.

"I know that you've been hurt, my dear, but I will make it right!"
Thus promising to "save" him, she defused his urge to flight.
"I promise you our love will last a century or more,
That you, and you alone, are what I've long been waiting for!"
"Oh no, no!" said the little Mark, who knew it was a lie,
That once inside her lair, 'twas clear - his fate would be to die.

Said the cunning Spinster to the Mark, "You must let go and trust
That what I want is what you want, and wish to do, and must."
While to herself she said, "What luck! To find a man like you,
Traumatized sufficiently to believe my words are true."
"Oh no, no!" said the little Mark, "I know this is a lie!
You want me to impregnate you, and then for me to die!"

The Spinster thought unto herself, if only he were dumb,
Though with sufficient poison, she was sure he would succumb.
So to him feigned a love that was as passionate as fire,
Convincing him, against his will, her wants were his desire.
"I fear you, gentle lady, for your sickly words seduce me,
But my instincts make it clear to me to that which they'll reduce me."

The Spinster kept the bombs of love careening through the air,
And, convinced her lies would do the trick, enticed him to her lair.
She wove a very subtle web, to steal from him his sperm -
To claim her single motherhood, then squash him like a worm.

She prattled on and on about their love, which was immortal!
Till she'd squeezed what little strength was left him deep inside
her portal -
Rejoicing now, 'twas clear she wouldn't need him as a father,
And could toss him on a heap, upon which none would ever
bother.

Alas, alas! The fate she had in store for this poor fool!
To steal from him his daughter, in acts most vile and cruel -
To cram that daughter's head with thoughts concealing what
she'd taken,
To glut her mind with pois'nous dreams from which she'd ne'er
awaken.
Up jumped the cunning Spinster, now the IVF was done -
She licked her lips, with smile most vile - her battle had been
won!
Rejoicing she had found a Mark she could now disembowel,
She set about to counsel that poor child in ways most foul.

And now, dear little children, who may this story read,
To false and evil scams and ploys, I pray you ne'er give heed!
When confronted with a lethal lying predator and shark,
Take a lesson from this tale, of the Spinster and the Mark.

The un-credible shrinking man

There's an ache within my heart I can't dispel -
I can't foresee its triggers, though I think I know its source -
Eventually it simply takes its course,
But while it has me in its grip, my life's a living hell.

Given this, I've seen my share of shrinks,
The one worse than the next, or so it's always seemed to me -
Their first and foremost focus is their fee -
The last thing on their mind is what their patient feels or thinks.

They claim it's a disorder of my mood,
A chemical imbalance or a product of my genes -
I do not know what any of that means,
Other than Big Pharma with psychiatrists collude.

If this were all to do with just my brain,
All their interventions wouldn't prove so insubstantial -
But their concern's primarily financial -
The patient's just a resource for pecuniary gain.

At best, they're shooting pricey, harmless blanks,
Though often they'll prescribe you things that with your health
will screw -
They know full well the hell you might go through,
But that does not distress them as they laugh their way to banks.

If you're in pain that's first and foremost mental,
Which eats away at you, or even threatens your existence,
I suggest from shrinks you keep your distance -
The damages that they inflict are often monumental.

Perhaps I am naïve or sentimental,
But I'm convinced there's something that is far more
fundamental -

Psychic anguish is environmental,
Frequently the outcome of abuse, likely parental.
I've seen this time and time again,
and have become judgmental -
People aren't born this way, it's all developmental.

The wannabe psychologist

I hear that you're headed to graduate school, and intend to become a psychologist,
But your teachers will see what you're made of the moment you open your mouth in their class -
Why not abandon this foolhardy quest, and study to be a proctologist?
At least there's a chance that you'll learn how it was that your head got so far up your ass.

The classes are small - it might take a semester, but likely will happen much faster -
They'll see that you're clueless, are clearly unhinged, and are selfish, sadistic and cruel -
A harpy, a hellcat, a mean girl on steroids, a blockbuster cruise ship disaster -
It's a given your teachers will all get your number, and throw you the hell out of school.

And what do you think will become of you then, when you're faced with your own constitution?
It's a given you'll start to break down, to implode, and to find that you're now underwater -
That you're empty inside, that it's always been so - you're a frivolous, vain Lilliputian
About to decompensate badly, and sure to succumb to your eating disorder.

But that will be only the start of your woes, as your "boyfriend" begins to see clearly
All your lies and deceptions, your vileness and malice, the things that you are and are made of -
That this was all fraudulent stagecraft, most artfully crafted, and that he has been merely
Your stooge, mark, and victim, whose future with you is a thing he ought be quite afraid of.

By the end of your twenties, you'll end up alone, in a cesspool of
major depression -
Your beau will have run for the hills, much relieved, by the time
that you're hitting the skids -
You'll be phoning your brand-new psychologist constantly,
hoping to squeeze in a session,
In which you'll complain you're a sexless, old spinster, who'll
never succeed or have kids.

Is it possible there could be anything worse than a world in
which you are a mother?
How could responsible people observe and allow it, to idly stand
by
As they watched all the barbarous forms of abuse you'd engage
in, one after the other?
The hope is you won't find a mate, are infertile, or, barring the
two of those, die.

The yearnings of furtive birds...

The yearnings of furtive birds,
bulging, and swelling
in congealed chorales -
The shadows of furtive dancers,
stealthily stealing
through curdled meadows -
The reveries of hermit owls,
secretly scrawled in deserted churches,
where fervent nurses intone slurred prayers
behind dour curtains.

In the holy valley, the sun-drenched girls emerge,
to suck the warm pulp
from the curved and colored earth -
While weird birds,
perched on swollen bells,
intone urgent warnings.

From their sea-cradle they emerge,
the thirsty girls -
beguiling the nerved ruins,
which will chill their lustful loins with a shrill wind,
and veil them in a dull shawl.

Now the felt foam surges no longer
through the parched throats of thirsty girls,
tossed from cradle comfort to murky madness -
And swallowed, in silence,
by damned and bloated birds,
on cursed and blasted bells.

Thoughts at Fifty - A collection of aphorisms

Shards of wisdom in a dark wood, midway on our life's journey...
(cf. opening lines, Inferno)

Men name things they do not understand to console themselves in their ignorance.

Duplicitous flattery disables its receiver, and provides the giver with a delicious sense of his own moral superiority.

Sincere flattery inevitably carries within it a deep sense of resentment and envy.

We know the truth about those we love, as well as ourselves. And we also know that, were we to linger upon it for more than the odd, uncomfortable moment, it would be fatal.

If you would know your true feelings towards a friend or acquaintance, heed your reaction when they disappoint you.

One risks no disappointment in venerating a dead hero.

Man is indeed the measure of all things: he disdains his inferiors, and abases himself before his betters. It is, however, only his equals whom he despises.

Comfort is illusion; illusion is comfort.

The "memoirist" requires an audience with whom to collude in his own self-deception.

The resentment and neediness of children too little loved masquerade later in life as their philosophies and religious convictions.

It is, in general, wise to take seriously the opinions of others in inverse proportion to the stubbornness with which they hold them.

Charitable acts often, nay, usually, incur the additional cost of their beneficiary's humiliation.

Received wisdom should be handled gingerly (to minimize the risk of infection), and promptly returned, unopened, to its sender.

Clever persons are rarely clever enough to discern how unappealing others find their cleverness.

It profits one little to advise those born without arms to seize the day.

A good novel is intrinsically pornographic. He who would deny it writes and/or reads bad novels.

Salomé's love is obsessive, yes, but only in degree and not in kind.

Nations are like individuals: they incessantly and quite unconsciously revise their own histories - to erase their evil deeds, and to assuage their consciences.

Those who profess to best know you have merely had more time in which to crystallize their own projections.

Unless and until you encounter an acquaintance in a novel setting, you can have no idea what you truly feel about them.

If you wish to be certain of never understanding something, name it. Or, better yet, unthinkingly adopt the one others have given it.

If you wish to be sure an acquaintance will never read a certain book, take care to recommend it to him or her.

Blessed be the meek - unless, heaven forbid, they inherit the earth - for then there will be all manner of hell to pay.

The recipient of a charitable deed is apt to attack as violently and unpredictably as an injured animal. Corollary: stay at least one step ahead of the walking wounded.

Those who would have you "surrender the self" will happily steal yours from you.

Powerful men have but one real conviction: that destiny has chosen them. Any others which they claim to possess are fictions.

Only blockheads, con-men, and cowards have firm convictions.

Young people are not wrong in feeling and behaving as if they were immortal. Their mistake lies in their confusion of their own individual existences with the boundless and eternal life-force pulsing within them.

Most men have an aversion to killing, but very little to allowing others be killed.

Young people find death fascinating. May they live long enough to feel differently.

There are those who find you quite as absurd as those whom you deem to be so.

What would a man beholden to no one do? - die of boredom, poisoned with contempt.

"Wisdom" never survives close and repeated scrutiny. It thrives on novelty, distance and mystification.

Any man, who is sufficiently grandiose and pretentious to explain to others the "meaning" of a myth, is almost certainly an intellectual fraud.

People with many friends are invariably frivolous.

Thoughtfulness is mutable, hypocrisy changeless.

Apologies make for great theater.

For newness to emerge, in art, and in life, much that is old must perish. Yet after one has walked amongst oaks, what satisfaction is there in lichens?

The childlike trust and hope we place in a new acquaintance accurately presages the extent of our later bitterness.

Some prejudices are hard-won, the products of a lifetime of reflection.

Let us take care to lay absolutely no claims upon the living when we are gone.

The music-dramas of Wagner are amongst the most sublime masterworks of western culture. Yet, without their frequent passages of leaden boredom, they would be very much less great. How to explain this?

We romanticize oblivion. But is it not, rather, the moments just prior to entering, and just after returning from it, that we cherish?

Pessimists are usually realists, hence useless. Only through some new, optimistic illusion does mankind make progress.

To designate a work or period of art "classic" is to say nothing substantive about it; it is merely an act of cultural and political narcissism.

Wisdom, in youth, concerns itself with *what*, so that, later in life, it might concern itself with *how*.

In practical or aesthetic discourse, one should steer a middle course between transparency and opacity, creating just enough mystery that one's listener believes that it can only be unraveled with his participation.

Life makes art possible; art makes life bearable.

There is no natural landscape which can compare with the one Beethoven evokes in his Pastoral symphony.

In worshipping heroes, one does not stand upon their shoulders, but rather cringes beneath their buttocks.

The man who professes his unpretentious nature unwittingly confesses his pretensions.

Flatter a man where he feels himself most vulnerable, if you would make of him your slave.

When a young person's lust fastens on a particular partner, the obsession to possess her troubles his thoughts, disrupts his sleep - in a word, overwhelms him. Her body becomes for him the mouthpiece through which the unborn express their previously mute craving for life. Their genius (Nature's genius) consists in clothing this craving in what the lover perceives as his own self-interest.

Whatever else she may or may not be, the evil stepmother, in fairy tales, represents the morally barren claims of the elderly upon resources rightfully belonging to the unborn.

Promiscuity is indeed a moral issue, but not in the prosaic and puritanical way in which it is usually framed.

People who cry at weddings do so from naïveté and/or self-pity.

What passes for "honesty" is often mere laziness, boorishness, and/or sadism.

Conceal your wishes from those whom you would have do your bidding.

Nature exults in destruction. Buried beneath the infant's intoxicating gurgles and coos echo the agonies and death-rattles of all its ancestors.

In disputes, the admission of a mistake, fault or, most effectively, character flaw (whether real or simply fabricated for the occasion) reliably disarms one's opponent.

Excessive subtlety usually masks a corresponding vapidity. What is worth saying can be said simply.

The average critic's grasp of a masterwork is akin to a gnat's sense of its surroundings, when it has unwittingly alighted upon a monument.

You will learn far more about great works by trying and failing to write one than by reading everything which has ever been written about them.

At the end of the rainbow one finds hope, a mischievous harlot.

One often steps through the manicured portico of a palace, only to find oneself in a dark and musty hovel.

Behind virtue invariably lurk vanity and pride.

What is commonly called goodness is usually simple indolence and/or timidity.

Humility is poorly disguised arrogance.

All pity is self-pity.

One's wisdom is only the accidental course of one's life clothed in haughty rhetoric.

Those who lament the decline of civilization, and/or the demise of culture, express only their anxiety at the prospect of their individual annihilation, and their rage towards their own creative impotence.

Those who would assure you that all is flux and process are, in fact, asking forgiveness for their inability to produce anything substantive and lasting.

Power does not corrupt so much as reveal man's true nature, when he no longer need grovel nor fear reprisal. Most men are Neros, lacking only in opportunity.

The weak and impotent would have us deem them "gentle".

How natural, easy, and yet how very foolish to declare slumbering passions dead.

Crisis reveals our character, above all to ourselves. How ironic that it is only our final struggle with death which will reveal our entire character to ourselves, when such knowledge is no longer of any use to us.

Most people lack the imagination to infer an inner life in others equal in richness and vulnerability to their own.

One fans others' affection and interest by the intermittent and unpredictable distribution of crumbs.

Those who claim to have no fear of death convince no one, least of all themselves, though that is their only purpose.

Those whom fate has forced to give birth to themselves are capable of an objectivity denied others, though they are vulnerable to cynicism, arrogance, and pride.

The number of repeated exposures which an artwork can survive, and still remain fresh and compelling, is a very precise indicator of its worth.

We prefer a single mediocre epiphany of our own to any number of demonstrably profound insights of others.

A group of effete homosexual aristocrats lounge about, and smugly attempt to best one another in a series of metaphysical pissing contests. If this seems to you a propitious environment in which to seek life's deepest truths, read Plato.

How very sad is the Tower of Babel tragedy of twentieth century music. And yet, amidst this din of solipsistic gibberish, it is our responsibility to listen, patiently and attentively. For prophets did once, and will again, come.

Contempt is a potent emotional aphrodisiac.

To cooly contradict one's opponent both provokes and unnerves him. He unwittingly shows his hand, and you have wagered and revealed nothing.

Skullcaps house intolerant and deeply frightened minds.

If you are naïve enough to believe in justice, you have never stood, accused and helpless, before a judge - subject to his perverse and momentary whim, and with his jackboot pressed firmly against your throat.

Every lawyer should undergo a period of incarceration, every physician one of serious illness.

We extol the individual - we make of them heroes, kings, martyrs, saints, messiahs… And yet it is apparent to anyone who has seriously considered the matter, that nature cares nothing at all for individuals.

Astronomers inform us that the universe is mostly empty space. Honest introspection reveals the same.

The paradox of music: it is only the repetition of recognizable material, within a given piece, which can persuade a listener to return to it.

How much gallantry and coquetry the lovers display in their attempt to hide from one another what they truly are! The species demands no less.

All of tragic literature is as nothing next to a single cry of a suffering child.

Novels temporarily engage us with the illusion that the world is not fundamentally ludicrous.

We belatedly notice the compartment into which the roulette ball has dropped, and proudly declare it our decision.

We maintain, in a later life, a special fondness for the music we loved at the onset of adolescence. Sadly, most adolescents are blockheads.

How rare it is that music escapes the egotistical indulgences and posturings of its composers and performers!

It is difficult for imaginative and/or introspective persons to live authentically; the temptation, even reflex, to fabricate their own novelistic portrayal of themselves is often too great.

A man's praise limits its object to the confines of his own understanding.

Men measure others against their own strengths and weaknesses, and deem such judgments objective.

Art is like the countenance of a beautiful woman, better admired from afar.

A happy man must necessarily lack the capacity for compassion.

Authentic hearts do not grow on sleeves.

To willingly lose an argument requires both great patience and great cunning.

The subtlest and most effective flattery requires its receiver to think it accidental.

Scenes from childhood often flood the minds of men approaching death; it is only then that they recognize that the interim of their adult life has been a vain and ephemeral dream.

We revere the dead, not least because their presence no longer threatens our vanity.

A man's most horrific nightmare has more intrinsic fascination for him than his greatest waking pleasure - for, in dream, man is God himself.

The path to a true friend's house is never strewn with eggshells.

The blockhead invariably wins any argument in which he engages.

Those who encourage one to turn the other cheek are merely desirous of the company of a fellow coward.

Love lies a remark away from hatred, and a few centimeters from disgust.

No happiness covers the cost of its own cessation.

Someday that bulb that burns out unexpectedly will be you.

On the countenances of the newly dead one finds written no revelations.

Contempt worthy of the name is a private matter.

Haughty demeanors are masks worn by cowards.

Truth is like the human form - it is most seductive when partially clothed.

How to explain men's delight in complaint? For men of sense, who know full well that it makes their company loathsome, find it well nigh impossible to forgo the pleasure it affords them.

A man with strong convictions is a fool, one with the courage of his convictions a dangerous fool.

Orthodoxy: a safe haven for bigots, blockheads and cowards.

The opinions of stubborn men are unwitting confessions of fear.

The net of language rarely catches a living fish.

When studying the wisdom of ancient sages, it is well to recall that they drank, ate, pissed, and shat exactly as you do.

The artistic impulse can consist of as little as the intuition that this or that bit in the work of another might have gone somewhat differently.

Uninterrupted magnificence, beauty, and eloquence invariably become tedious.

Most people are like popular songs - their charms are, perhaps, momentarily diverting, but they invariably wilt upon repeated exposure.

The frivolity and savagery of life should hardly surprise us, when we stop for a moment to consider the nature of the act from which it arises.

Trauma survivors are the emotional aristocrats of the world.

Self-loathing is self-love by another name.

Only healthy men with full bellies complain of their psychological and emotional distress.

Every nitwit has the courage of his convictions - how much nobler and braver for a man to cast them aside, and look upon the world with the eyes of a child!

The certainty that life is random, chaotic, and ultimately meaningless is as asinine a religious dogma as any other.

To celebrate a wedding is akin to celebrating a victory prior to a competitive sporting event.

The world of adults is one in which the corpses of children marry, procreate, conduct business, and finally die a second time.

If a man holds you in a penetrating and unflinching gaze upon first meeting you, he is not to be trusted.

A man who reads for pleasure generally does not live for it.

Popular music brings much mischief and misery into the world, with its cheap and vulgar promises of idealized love.

The consolation of aging: to no longer be subject to the tyranny of one's loins.

Books, radios, televisions, films, telephones, cyberspace, et al. - human beings prefer almost anything to the proximate company of their neighbors.

The frequency of lovers' protestations is proportionate to their subliminal understanding that the present state of their love is doomed.

If you would be taken for an original, take care to plagiarize with judicious subtlety.

Intellectuals inspect inanimate matter in the hope that they might experience the delicious ecstasy of snuffing out whatever small speck of life they may chance to happen upon, once and for all.

Arguments about the acoustical "unnaturalness" of atonal music are particularly specious in an age of genetic engineering. Art is not, and never has been, "natural".

Teachers are understandably reticent to confess to their students that nothing worth learning can be taught.

The intolerance and rage automobile drivers routinely feel for one another are merely their authentic feelings towards others, sans the threat of physical and/or social repercussion, i.e., in anonymity, man is a rageful and contemptuous beast.

What a curious fellow, the prolific misanthrope! For whom does he write?

Addenda

The man who delights in the outer lives of others has no inner life of his own.

The man who ardently professes his love of god and/or country unwittingly confesses his own inner emptiness and self-loathing.

Were youth to suddenly possess the wisdom of age, all the hectic, meaningless bustle of the world, as well as all innovation, would cease.

All artistic admiration depends upon the intellectual inferiority of the admirer. To a cleverer god, ours would surely seem a bungler.

A professional is someone who has so deadened his sensibility with specialized knowledge and received wisdom that he no longer recognizes anything other than his own prejudices; he perceives all innovations as threats, all passion as naïveté and affectation. Vive le dilettante!

One is as likely to find wisdom in recently penned or spoken words as in a chance encounter with a blockhead on a walk. If you would be wise, search both space and time, even-handedly, for wisdom.

When a man is thrown back upon himself, i.e., sans distraction, stimulation, or immanent need, he is soon bored. Boredom is man's naked encounter with the intrinsic nullity of existence.

In supermarkets, amoral blockheads wander hungrily through vacuum-packed Rwandas.

An icy temperament invariably reveals its watery origins under proper conditions.

Any new perspective or experience which enables one to take life less seriously is by definition a piece of wisdom.

In contemplating a particular profession, it is instructive to observe its elderly practitioners. What it has given to and taken from them is inevitably inscribed upon their countenances.

Regard the man who listens attentively with care: he is either utterly depraved, or truly noble.

Tragedy errs in elevating the absurdities of life and death into matters of life and death.

Frivolity and dissipation are unwitting philosophical positions, worthy of serious consideration.

Music - created by monsters and performed by narcissists, tyrants, and slaves, bathed in sweat and trombone spittle, and yet... divine.

A messiah is merely the subsequent monster who has not yet arrived, and/or the conveniently martyred totem upon whom monsters enthrone themselves.

Much of parents' disapproval of and/or rage towards their children is merely their dim and deeply envious intuition that those children inhabit an enchanted world, to which they are no longer privy.

The writer of ugly music unwittingly betrays his own rage and emotional stinginess.

Art is most often created and treasured by depressives. Is it any wonder that art which gives pleasure appears to them either suspicious or unworthy?

Rosenkavalier is superior to Elektra - and the sheer red-blooded pleasure one takes in it is no small part of why.

No one experiences their own mortality as real who has not yet suffered the loss of a loved one. And it is precisely at this point that childhood ends.

To blame the victim is a cruel and foolish thing. And yet it conceals, hidden and much distorted, a very subtle truth: every victim is a victim of necessity, i.e., their fate could not have been other than it was. How far all this lies from childish notions of karma and morality...

The road to contentment is strewn with diminished expectations and discarded desires.

We have intimate, privileged, and immediate access to our own mental and physical sufferings - yet how little we know of who and what we are! Our character is revealed to us only gradually, through the judicious observation of our own behavior.

There are no happy endings, only temporary reprieves.

Life and thought are contingent and determined. So too are our opinions and choices.

Your opinions are only transparent masks for your own petty insecurities. They make you miserable, and cause others to hate you.

Between the three or four moments of inspiration, and the countless functions of respiration, digestion, and elimination, which constitute a man's life, lies the true measure of his existence.

Ripeness in a man is that rarely yet potentially productive moment between naïveté and corruption.

Programmatic depictions of nature in music become just so many narcissistic noodlings in those moments when one hears the authentic voice of nature herself.

We are grateful to philosophers for their compelling claims re the nullity and vanity of existence, for we do not disdain truth - yet how much more grateful we are to those who help make it bearable by bringing beauty and laughter into the world.

Thoughts re my birth and eventual death

To begin with, I was born.

Well, not exactly. To begin with, I was a sudden speck of viscous flotsam- an unwilling proto-consciousness, wandering through the ether, stuck in a mucous-filled soup of brine and foulness, in which enraged corpuscles struggled through nauseating, gelatinous bubbles of reluctantly fast-forming flesh, tails, and fins - the recalcitrant ancestor of every absurd creature that has ever sloshed, swam, walked, or flown through or over this slimy green ball of one-celled slop, plankton, ooze, sperm, dung, and decay. Then suddenly there was this vile catheter in my navel, squirting mother's plasma, junk food, over-mentholated Marlboro cigarettes, and vulgarity into me like a cheap colostomy bag turned inside out. Where was I a moment ago? Before this infernal, warm, slushy stew surrounded me, suffocated me, and eventually belched me up out of a beloved nothing and nowhere into this blinding glare of piss, shit, vomit, and horrid racket? We are born between piss and shit, all of us. And to piss and shit we shall return. And in between? Piss and shit, with a few delightful additions - phlegm, vomit, sweat, spittle, stink. We are bags of water - bloated, over-fertilized, genetically modified potatoes with constantly jabbering mouths - slimy enemas, spat out from a divine void into a fiery Hell. Denizens of the deep.

I, too, am terrified of bad food - of eating it, of becoming it. I will sew my mouth shut with whatever I can lay my hands on - dental floss, picture wire, my vile mother's costume jewelry - anything to escape this inferno of boiling sludge.

Is there nowhere dry left to be found in this one-horse universe?

After I die, I intend to really get going with my life, know what I mean? As in - really take stock of my accomplishments, as objectively as I can, in as open and fair-minded a way as I can manage - those I loved, hated, helped, hurt, what I produced, what I regret not having produced, all that clichéd, St. Peter sort of crap. On second thought, why bother with any of that? I'll be floating in some delicious ether - all those Earth-bound yokels won't mean a damn thing to me. Fuck 'em.

I might check out my funeral, just to make sure everything's in order. I would imagine I'll be very much hoping that anyone who shows up, if anyone shows up, will be monumentally upset - that there will be an absolutely deafening wailing and gnashing of teeth, and that the funeral home will be thundering with earsplitting, heartfelt sobbing, shrieks, and bellows. This being the case, I MIGHT consider some sort of posthumous decree, which would, at least eventually, at some far-future date, allow them all to get over it, and get on with their lives. More likely not, since the comedy will be so priceless. Then again - fuck it. No funeral for me.

I will transform into a fiber-optic device the size of a molecule, and take careful note of all the important changes my having lived has wrought in the frontal lobes, neocortexes, hippocampi, limbic systems, and amygdalae of various and sundry individuals, to be named at a later date in a document I am presently preparing.

Yup, things will really pick up speed when I die. Since I will never have to waste any time eating, or taking a piss or shit, or any of the innumerable pointless and disgusting things meat puppets spend the bulk of their lives doing, I will have an enormous amount of leisure time. I will certainly have the time to spy on a wide variety of people, and, at least in a few cases, vanishingly few, wish them well - in other, that is to say, in most cases, I will wish them bad luck and misery of Herculean proportions - failure, loss, grief, illness, chronic pain, painful deaths, yada yada yada - you get the idea. Just kidding! Sort of.

I will astral travel to all of the awesome, natural wonders of the Earth, which I never had the nerve to visit in life because I was an introverted, hateful coward. But why restrict myself to earth? The universe shall be my oyster.

After I die, I will be privy to all the secret, inner workings of both time and space. I will undo and redo an infinite number of things. I will live a thousand simultaneous lives - Attila, Caligula, Ivan the Terrible, Vlad the Impaler, Sade, Kaspar

Hauser, Wagner, Hitler, Ted Bundy, Ryan Seacrest, a fetus in the womb of Elizabeth Báthory, if all those wonderful rumors about her are true, a fetus with the mind of an ancient, all-knowing being. They'll be absolutely no end to the horseplay and buffoonery in which I'll be indulging myself. You'll see! Hahaha - no, you won't.

I will observe the string that attaches the umbilical cord of all sentient beings, one to the other, dangling and shimmering like a celestial spider's web from an impossibly high cloud far above the Earth. And since I will have a refined sense of humor, which was utterly denied to me during my time on Earth, I shall laugh uproariously, from my newfound cosmic perspective, at all of life, at birth, at death. Hahaha! That will be me.

Time will freeze. I will observe the eleven dimensions of space as if they were a very large Nerf ball, manufactured for me, and me alone.

My music will stream and course like veins and rivers of lava, mucus, and blood through every nook and cranny of this shit-ball we call Earth, of the galaxy, of the entire universe, time permitting - leaving all those sentient beings who are privileged and/or unlucky enough to hear it tattooed with red-hot branding-irons, and left with body-wide, excruciating scars, which will remind them, for all eternity, who's the boss.

I will finally wake up and smell the coffee. Just metaphorically, of course.

I would watch my children grow, if I had had any, except for that one little piece of shit, who hates me passionately. Her I shall ignore, for blood is thicker than both formaldehyde and methanol. May those whom she has tortured and will doubtless torture in the future pay her back, but good. I shall demur.

Three wackadoodle rock 'n' roll song lyrics

I. Black wolves nippin'

Black wolves nippin' at your baldin' tires,
Framed in the shadows of the twilight gloom -
The blood in your coffee takes the shape of madness,
And boils off the carpet in your living room.

Barely dressed witches makin' change at strip malls,
Leanin' over counters with their cleavage out -
Laceratin' customers, whose innocent incompetence
Keeps 'em from perceivin' what they're talking about.

An innocent child whizzes by on a skateboard,
Laughin' loud and guileless in a dark green blouse -
Squealin' like an overly protective mother penguin,
Who's carryin' her children to the charnel house.

Purrin' like an oboe in a poorly played cantata,
Sketchin' black blossoms through the tinted glass -
Like the whispers of death at the end of a performance,
Like the driver of a hearse just run out of gas.

Fat babies nursin' at the Arboretum
In abandoned houses overrun with moss -
An old man wheezin' in the prickly-ass brambles,
Clingin' on to life, no matter what the cost.

On a gravelly path in the heart of the forest,
A contemptuous crow gives you pause for thought -
Your teeth are shakin' wildly, and your bones are tremblin' -
Whatever you might learn here's gonna be dearly bought.

There's a congregation there singin' gray Hosannas -
Rail-thin ladies sittin' in plush armchairs -
You're achin' from exhaustion, and a gnawin' sadness -
You ask 'em all for mercy - not a one of 'em cares.

The preacher says the end of the world is at hand,
While an old crone whispers and the piano player sighs -
He starts in to cacklin' 'bout fire and brimstone,
Babblin' on 'bout Satan bein' the King of Lies.

Crows shreikin' insults from an oaken cross -
Red mud glintin' in a mindless dawn -
It's too early for supper and too late for suicide -
There ain't no sense in asking favors from old friends who are
gone.

I bend to kiss a flower, catch my lip on a thorn -
The braggin' of the blackbirds make my insides sad -
A woman sings a lullaby to nobody it seems,
Or maybe to a child she mighta loved, but never had.

Sufferin's a given, but knowledge is elective -
Minist'rin' to children, who are seekin' grace -
Feedin' 'em with pebbles from polluted rivers -
They're lookin' for salvation, but they're in the wrong place.

Time don't heal - that's an old wives' tail -
Just the promise of death, and the solace of art -
A fire in the brain, or a sudden desire -
It don't make up for everything, but it's a start.

II. Docked and loaded

I smell stale cigar smoke in the ocean breeze -
I got some dark blue welts from a jellyfish sting -
I got hydrochloric acid coming out my mouth -
My doppelgänger just sits there - he don't say a thing.

Read me a story - tell me a lie -
Throw a deep, green mattress on a flower bed -
Toss me a blanket, then tell me the truth -
Cuz I don't buy one single word of what you just said

Chorus

<I hear lonely sirens singin' in a house of cards -
I see lungfish walkin' on feet of clay -
I hear pedophilic preachers on the cable news
Goin' on and on 'bout the Judgment Day.>

I never really had a friend like you before -
I don't mingle with the crowd, or with other musicians -
You can say what you want, but you're gonna do what I say,
Cuz it's me that's gonna lay down all the terms and conditions.

Throw me a party - toss me a bone -
Quit your singin' and your beggin' on those cold city streets -
Blow me a bubble - drop me a line -
Then tell me 'bout your politics between the sheets.

Chorus

I hear lonely sirens, etc.

III. Right fine day

There's a fatal vision in the lungs of time -
A bestial-ass dance on the Earth's wide wound,
A porous hole in the belly of Justice,
A crack in the cradle of the crescent moon.

Meet me at noon by the Governor's tombstone -
I'll give ya five whole minutes in which to make your case,
Then put your lame-ass problems on a twilit trolley,
And get your sorry ass out my fuckin' face.

Chorus

<Oh well, it's a right fine day -
There ain't a single cloud in the morning sky -
There ain't no place to run to, and nothin' to whine about -
I picked a right fine day on which to die.>

Whisper my name over the stale wind's shoulder,
Then throw my stinkin' corpse on a pile of dung -
Mock every damn thing that I once treasured,
Then bury the rope from which I'm hung.

Or shove me back through the gates of Eden,
And close me up in the Earth's wide womb -
Shuffle me off to a nice, safe place
In a cosy, cushy coffin 'neath a high-end tomb.

Chorus

Oh well, it's a right fine day, etc.

Tiny plants once ruled the seas

Tiny plants once ruled the seas,
Like mem'ries in an aging brain -
Spittle in and spittle out -
The menace of a quiet rain

Which whispers things that burn like fire,
Like ants on skin, which chill the blood
Of generations long since gone -
Fossils in the sunbaked mud

Which borders lakes, upon which men
Have set their hopes and fragile hearts,
Which break like shells in frying pans,
In faux-dramatic fits and starts.

The engines of the future hum
Like playful phantoms, mouthing words
Of bawdy tunes they learned as girls
From messianic prophet birds

On hungry trees and tinderboxes,
Set aflame by hired hands -
Washed and shaken to their core
By drums of war in distant lands

Where blows for freedom to one's head
Rule the body politic -
The time draws near - the id's unleashed -
The ego crumbles brick by brick.

Step by step, the autumn leaves -
The countryside grows white and still -
The townsfolk grasp their deep remorse,
And gloomily descend the hill

To occupy the promised land -
Disperse the teeming, yearning hordes
With drones of sheer monotony
And plowshares turned back into swords

Which plunge into the clouds above,
Visible to acolytes
And desert monks in snazzy hair shirts,
Flying multicolored kites

Across the vaulted dome of heaven -
Cross your hearts, and hope to die -
Across their folded middle fingers,
Hidden to conceal the lie

Lurking in the earth's wide bosom -
Buckled up, and battened down -
Hatched in gray assembly lines,
Where bold ideas and sorrows drown

In fairy dust, in cups of tea,
Which boil off impurities
Of failing fast and fallen angels -
A pinch of snuff, a random sneeze -

The pollen hanging in the air
Coats windpipes in the throats of men,
Who scarcely had a chance to live
Before their souls were born again

To parents in delivery rooms,
The world seems bright and incandescent -
To those who've been around the block
The traffic's thick, the noise incessant.

Leave your firearms at the door -
Spread your cards out on the table -
Look the devil in the eye,
If you're willing and you're able.

Bodies come, and bodies go,
Though ugliness is to the bone -
You will not find a gentle spirit
In a vengeful, spiteful crone.

Ease up on the masochism -
Put aside your hard-won guilt -
Lay aside your crown of thorns
Before your store-bought roses wilt.

The chambermaid is off today -
The butler's passed out in his room -
Explore the mansion quickly now!
To dawdle is to spell your doom.

Two heinous women

Two heinous women in a house full of crap
They hope and pray will shield them from pain -
Nourish them, preserve them, and insure that they'll be safe -
A fantasy they desperately maintain -

Which fosters in the two of them the laughable conceit
That they are always right, and you? Mistaken -
Up close this was repellent, from a distance 'twas a farce -
But now I am phlegmatic and unshaken -

For once you see your enemies are utterly ridiculous,
You're free! They cannot touch you in the least -
The power of those miscreants to make life living hell
Has withered on the vine, and finally ceased.

I used to have the wish that they be bound upon a spit -
Gagged, and tied, and lashed, each to the other -
And as they slowly barbecued, I'd chuckle as I watched
The little one die first, and then her mother.

I never think about that now - I'll leave that for another -
What I do now is close my ears, and let them
Puke up all the bile that the two of them can muster -
Their words are simply words, and I forget them

Sooner than some mildly unpleasant sort of dream,
Which one cannot recall upon arising -
So trivial, so trifling, and completely idiotic
No shrink would find it worth the analyzing -

Which, truth to tell, I tried to do far longer than I should have,
For I was stunned that beings like this existed -
Unconscious, hateful hags, without a shred of empathy that might have
Helped me make my exit unassisted.

All my friends and fam'ly reassured me I was right -
They were simply scum, and best ignored -
Beastly Lilliputians who deserved, at best, disdain,
Which seemed a waste of time and left me bored -

For there was no one home for whom it paid to give a thought,
Not least the one to whom I once was wed -
'Twas long ago I took that ring, threw it in a ditch,
And grew to loathe them both, and wish them dead.

But now that I am free, if I'm aware of them at all,
They don't arouse a shred of real concern -
And when some Grand Inquisitor consigns them to the stake,
I will not waste my precious time to watch those witches burn.

When I was a boy

When I was a boy,
The lake was a primitive, cool blue -
Sedimentary, my dear Watson -
Dead, more likely -
With barely a flicker
On the MRI
From its frontal lobes -
All the while,
The over-earnest researchers
Humped
Nervously and furiously
In the adjacent locker room.

On the far shore,
Mermaids pleasured themselves
With spent Fukushima rods,
Smiling through cancer-ravaged faces,
As their red hair fell from their scalps
To ride the crisp autumn breeze
Towards Hell-camps
Of barnacled televangelists
Singing barcarolles
To their syphilitic mistresses
In bombed-out Mississippi motels.

Fragments of a life -
Misspelled,
Unchecked,
Bowdlerized,
And shouted from rooftops to no one in particular...

In Mauritania,
Newly pubescent girls
Are force-fed until they become diabetic,
Often dying from heart failure in the process -
But that's not the secret I wanted to share.

Got a light?
Any standard-issue blowtorch will do -
Listen...
Charlie Parker has climbed the magnificent oak tree in the park -
He's twelve again,
As yet unspoiled,
A mere eighteen inches tall,
Eagerly practicing,
On the verge of discoveries
That will change jazz forever -
How sweet!
A woodpecker has fastened a Do Not Disturb sign,
And is offering free smack and syringes
To anyone who can sing back an entire chorus after just one
hearing.

My dog makes up for much of what is horrible in life,
But he may very well leave before I -
Although it's just as likely I will snuff it first -
And then what?
Perhaps I'll take a shine to Geritol,
Or the poems of Charles Bukowski,
Perhaps the newest acid reflux medication,
Obscure outtakes from Kubrick's films -
More likely
I'll avail myself
Of Starbucks' soon-to-be-unveiled offer of free cyanide capsules
With their double espresso.

What makes you say being a schizo-affective, manic-depressive
Is not a freely chosen postmodern lifestyle?
Oh yes, that...
Well, that IS a bit hard to explain -
In any event, I'll return the power drill in the morning,
Once I've hung the Photoshopped Munch painting,
Drained the kitty pool of chlorine,
And replaced it with arsenic-laced estrogen
In anticipation of next Sunday's barbecue.

But now I'm a man,
Way past forty-six -
And have replaced my childhood dreams
With adult illusions -
Ha ha, not really -
Rather a walking corpse,
A dusty springfield
Void of crops -
A black hole,
A bit of Hawking radiation,
A veritable Republican,
A faulty synapse,
An unemployed poltergeist,
Traveling light
Through the ruins
Of an abandoned particle zoo.

Good night, Irene -
Do let the Bonobos sleep in tomorrow morning!
They've had a rough week.

When your neutered dogs dick...

When your neutered dog's dick
Shoots out into space
Like a Cassini probe
In search of a bacchanalian proctological exam,
Change is in the wind -
Rubber-gloved deities
Exchange phone numbers and bodily fluids
In darkened choir stalls,
Spied upon
By guilt ridden clerics,
And ransacked
By bad cops gone good -
I tawt I taw a puddy tat today -
A mangy, monstrous, saber-toothed warthog of a thing,
Performing cavity searches
Of indentured Rhinemaidens,
Who slave nights
Over faux-porcelain bidets,
Left unsanitized
By tidy men
In bowler hats
and unwashed tee shirts -
Long ago abandoned
By Italian grandfathers,
Roaming in Penthouse Forums
With abridged views,
And clearly up to no good -
Roughed out,
Patted down,
And sold down the river
By TSA scanners
Wearing cheap façades,
And crowing about their Hawking radiation-proof investments
Through their obviously unhygienic oxygen masks.

The world is a comedy for those who stink,
And a tragedy for those who must smell them.
No kissing in coach
Or petting in the cockpit!
Where olive-tinged scrotums
Melt in the mouths
Of platinum-haired stewardesses
On Mediterranean diets,
Planted in thick compost,
And freshly smeared
By dung-wielding immigrants
Listening to the White Album
On their shit-stained iPods.

Have a close friend lie to you
While massaging your gums,
And scraping damp steel wool over your heavily knitted brow -
While maniac spinsters
Plot eviscerating revenge on you
Out to the twelfth generation -
Hope they die before you get old.

When shall we three meet again?
Let's plan for the very next Council of Nicaea,
Or that inevitable, umpteenth Aerosmith farewell concert -
Barring that -
How about at the nurses' station after evening meds?
Though it would seem
The character of our collective tsuris
Now cleaves to the ward
Like a Jewish caricature,
Of interest only to elderly, conscience-ridden, former Third
Reich bodyguards,
And/or the most soulful of Creedmoor inmates -
Yes, that would be us -
You and I -
Without regard to race,
Color,
Whether one is up to speed,

Or has AARP discounted tickets to PBS sponsored classic-rock
shows,
Whose Horizons are either limitless,
Or partially covered by Blue Cross.

Your hearts hope to die
At or near the same time you do.
Ergo -
Choose Erykah Badu,
But well before her Urdu phase,
Before the Plague of Ebonics
Spread its freshly creamed cheese
In and throughout the svelte, sweaty thighs
Of a popular culture
Unknown before the sudden Byzantine advent of Greek yogurt,
Milked by shepherds,
And fermented by sleazy Madison Avenue types -
Their deadened souls
Raised on robbery,
And stacking staff-infested, ShopRite shelves
To the strains of rancid, honey-vanilla arrangements of
Woodstock -
Their peanut allergies
A long forgotten nightmare
Of their repressed childhoods,
In which both underwear and regimes
Were changed brutally,
And with no notice -
The 120 days of Saddam -
Buckled up,
Hunkered,
And bunkered down in a crepuscular crevice -
A fissured fistula,
In which no self-respecting fishmonger would care to cast his
couch
With either snug or ill-fitting garments -
The subject of nasty gossip
Of pill-popping matrons,

Shut away in more or less lenient districts
By obese administrators

When you see mortality in a blade of grass -
Terror?
Vertigo?
Pick-up or delivery?
Brown rice with that?
The park itself comes undone,
Unglued -
The bees mushroom to prehistoric size -
The mushrooms lie poisonous and hysterical
In the choked breeze -
The dog knows full well,
Sniffed it out ages ago -
But he is as resigned as you are not.
You would wiggle your way into that woodpecker hole
Were you tiny enough -
And were it not maggot-infested,
You would paint warnings in the sky
With the once full stream of your adolescent bladder if you
could -
(were there anyone sufficiently ripe
to read and understand them)
Better to dribble your piss
In a fast-melting snow,
Engorged and prostrate
To no one in particular -
To the well-sinewed sweat and spunk
Of a past
You barely remember.

The end times are coming -
Maybe for all,
But definitely for you.
Put a pot on the stove -
I hear Persephone enjoys herbal teas from China -
All of them, in fact -

Her depression has made of her a promiscuous drunkard,
Though high-functioning -
That is to say:
She will not be dissuaded from or forget her purpose in coming -
Nor will the acrid mothballs
You've placed carefully around the perimeter of your house
Serve to distract her -
Not to mention,
The moths have all recently evolved
To eat them without harm anyway -
On the way to your garments -
On the way to your guts -
No glory -
No Hallelujahs or Hosannas -
No overpriced Neiman Marcus hosiery.

Sock your cash away in a bedbug-infested mattress -
Your earthly treasure -
You can take it with you
On a leisurely bike ride
To your Last Supper,
Where it will be put in a collection plate
And fed to worms
On a strict probiotic diet
Of angst and flesh -
Darker and darker the night -
More and more insipid the grins of those who choose not to
notice -
This world is not all!
It cannot possibly be all!
The sheer, intolerable, brute stupidity
That we would be forced to face
Were it to be so,
Proves that it is not -
I undid the laces from my water boots,
Threw them over a rafter,
And then froze,
Cold as ice.
But God didn't want that -

Not exactly that, at any rate -
He's after something quite other.

At the end of the bardos, there is no rainbow,
Only an unassuming lemonade stand
Operated by a lonely, little blonde-haired girl
Whose face is hidden behind angelic curls
And a deeply bowed head -
Thirsty,
Exhausted,
Death-drunk,
Expecting nothing...

Don't pull that goddamn sword from the tree!
It only prolongs the awful sitcom
You wish you had never turned on in the first place -
There's static in the attic,
In the foyer -
And the living room has become a makeshift mausoleum -
Grandma would have cropped the dog's ears,
Had the cats not eaten her first.

The dog -
Of course!
The dog -
He sits regally on the futon,
Not a thought in his head -
The incarnation of Charlemagne,
The signatory of doom.

When your neutered dog's dick
Sticks out like a bad cop's nightstick
In a dark alley
Of a minority neighborhood,
Change is in the wind -
Its rhythm rises
In the honey-suckled cradles
Of myopic streets -

Through dark lashes
Worn down by underaged girls
In svelte penthouses,
Where potted plants and parted ways
Pant heavily
In ripped nets
Of embarrassed fishermen,
Blinded by greed,
Lust,
And the savage idols of their youth.

In Asia, careers grow on trees -
Men languish away
With bellies full of low-hanging fruit,
And the lonely hearts of suffocating lungfish,
Mangled and stomped upon
By the bound feet
Of illiterate poets -
Poets like me,
Unborn and grasping.

About the Author

Philip Traum was born and bred in New England, and has been writing poetry since his teenage years. After an ill-fated second marriage, Philip emigrated to Newfoundland, where he lives, tranquilly and contentedly, with his beloved dog, Parker; his books, scores, and Steinway piano; and the ever-present memories of his first wife, Cathy.

www.ingramcontent.com/pod-product-compliance
Lightning Source LLC
Chambersburg PA
CBHW051723040426

42447CB00008B/945